THE WEB CONTENT STYLE GUIDE

An Essential Reference for Online Writers, Editors, and Managers

GERRY MCGOVERN

ROB NORTON

CATHERINE O'DOWD

An imprint of Pearson Education

London · New York · San Francisco · Toronto · Sydney
Tokyo · Singapore · Hong Kong · Cape Town · Madrid
Paris · Milan · Munich · Amsterdam

PEARSON EDUCATION LIMITED

Head Office:
Edinburgh Gate
Harlow CM20 2JE
Tel: +44 (0)1279 623623
Fax: +44 (0)1279 431059

London Office:
128 Long Acre
London WC2E 9AN
Tel: +44 (0)20 7447 2000
Fax: +44 (0)20 7240 5771
Website: www.business-minds.com

First published in Great Britain in 2002

ISBN: 0 273 65605 8

British Library Cataloguing in Publication Data
A CIP catalogue record for this book can be obtained from the British Library.

10 9 8 7 6 5 4 3 2 1

Typeset by Pantek Arts Ltd, Maidstone, Kent
Printed and bound in Great Britain by Biddles Ltd, Guildford and King's Lynn

The Publishers' policy is to use paper manufactured from sustainable forests.

ACKNOWLEDGEMENTS

Screenshots on pages 28, 86, 227, 231 reprinted by permission from Microsoft Corporation. Screenshots on pages 228 reprinted by permission from Thomas Crosbie Media. Screenshot on page 196, reprinted by permission from Google Inc. Screenshots on pages 19, 88, reprinted by permission from Amazon.com, Inc. Screenshots on pages 170, 229 reprinted by permission from Salon.com. Screenshots on pages 20, 70, 121 reprinted by permission from Yahoo! Inc. Screenshots on pages 23, 180 reprinted by permission from Iomega Corporation. Screenshot on page 112 reprinted by permission from IBM Corporation. Screenshots on pages 30, 155, 194 reprinted by permission from Dell Computer Corporation. Screenshots on pages 26, 78, 189 reprinted by permission from Cable News Network (CNN) LP, LLLP.

CONTENTS

Introduction vii

I **WRITING FOR THE WEB** 1

Shorter is better 2
Be direct 3
Web headings that work 5
Use subheads 7
Web paragraphs are different 8
Keep your sentences simple 9
Getting ready to write 11
Editing yourself 13
A final thought 15

II **DESIGNING FOR THE WEB** 17

Design for the reader 18
Every website is a directory 19
From getting attention to giving attention 21
Structure is boring, but it works 21
The Web is also like a newspaper 22
Web layout is simple layout 24
Web design is conventional design 27
Navigation and search are critical 28
Design for interactivity 30
Web design: keep it simple, structured, and reader-centric 31

III AN A TO Z OF WEB CONTENT STYLE 33

APPENDIX I: SAMPLE STYLE GUIDE 235

Language 235
Reference dictionaries and stylebooks 235
Usage 236
Word list/glossary 237

FURTHER READING/ONLINE RESOURCES 239

QUICK-FIND INDEX 243

INTRODUCTION

Good writing is the exception rather than the rule on the Web. One reason is simply that it's hard to write well. Another is that many of the people who've been involved with the Web from the beginning have been slow to realize that writing is a very big part of what the online experience is about. While the Web has important non-textual uses, such as listening to audio files, watching video files, and downloading software and music, most people who use it spend an overwhelming amount of their online time reading words on a page. It's not an accident that we call them web*pages*. Nor is it an accident that the language used to create webpages is called Hyper*text* Markup Language (HTML).

Following on from this logic, we call the person who comes to a website a *reader*. That doesn't mean they can't do other things on a website, such as purchase a product, download software, or listen to audio. It merely recognizes that the primary activity for the vast majority of people when they access the Web is *reading*. We also call a website a *publication* because, when you think about it, that's what a website is. A website publishes content targeted at a group of readers. "Reader" is a much warmer and more explanatory word than the generic "user." (Two things websites and illegal drugs have in common: they share the words "user" and "traffic.")

Writing, in fact, is arguably the most important link in the chain of devices, technologies, software, and interfaces that propels ideas across the Web—more important than the kinds of computer, operating system, browser software, or Internet connection method used. Writing is also the least understood link in that chain, and the one least likely to improve with technology.

Because the Web is accessed through a computer, many organizations assume it is something technical. What they fail to realize is that the Web is in fact a publishing medium, just like print. These organizations have put in place the technical infrastructure to publish webpages, but have rarely bothered to create the kind of editorial infrastructure that a publisher must have. One reason for this is that the people in charge of websites—webmasters, chief technology officers, chief information officers—tend to have quantitative backgrounds; they're more familiar with HTML and programming than with grammar and composition.

In addition to quality content, the design of websites must facilitate finding and reading that content. Web design is about laying out content so that it can be easily read. It's about organizing content so that it can be easily navigated and searched. For the vast majority of websites, design should *not* be about elaborate graphics and visual effects. The number-one design principle for the Web is simplicity. Quality web design should be all about making life easier for the reader to find content, and then making it easy for them to read that content.

As quality content becomes ever more critical in differentiating successful websites from others, the need for quality control will grow. Two things that the Web needs in general—and which every website needs in particular—are standards and rules.

While there will never be the kind of hard and fast rules about web publishing that there are about, say, web software, general standards are in fact emerging. The number of websites that are badly written, badly edited, and badly designed remains vast, but if you look at the successful, high-volume websites, you see professional editing and standard design.

About *The Web Content Style Guide*

This book aims to codify the rules and standards that make for effective web writing. It also aims to give non-technical guidance to all those involved in designing and running a website, from the chief executive officer to the junior writer. Its easy-to-access A to Z format makes it an ideal reference guide for all those involved in web publishing.

Many excellent style guides exist in the offline world. Three of the best known are the University of Chicago Press's *Manual of Style*, *The New York Times Manual of Style and Usage*, and the *Associated Press Stylebook and Briefing on Media Law*. Grammar and style issues are only one aspect of *The Web Content Style Guide*, and it focuses on those points particularly relevant to the Web as well as some of the more common pitfalls in grammar and usage. In this way, *The Web Content Style Guide* is a companion guide rather than an alternative to the established offline guides.

Some of the web grammar and style issues you will find here include

- the key differences between American and British English
- how the Web accentuates plagiarism
- the use of italics
- what sort of dash looks best on the screen
- and when and how to date documents

In the area of design and layout, *The Web Content Style Guide* examines topics from accessibility to animation, from fonts to forms, from information architecture to intranet, from navigation to newsgroup, and from search to style guides.

Every entry is written from the perspective that a website must get the right content to the reader as quickly as possible, in the most readable manner. The FONTS entry, for example, discusses the font sizes and types that work best on screen.

The book is organized into three sections:

- the Introduction, including an overview on writing and designing for the Web
- the A to Z index
- supplementary material comprising a sample style guide, a list of further reading/online resources, and a quick-find index

If you're involved in managing, designing, editing, or writing for a website, *The Web Content Style Guide* is essential for you. It is packed with examples, and is written in a clear, concise, and friendly manner. Based on the authors' 40-plus collective years of experience in traditional publishing, and 15 in designing content-rich websites, it is always practical. It champions best practices in web content writing, layout, and design, and is not afraid to kill off a few Internet myths along the way.

WRITING FOR THE WEB

I

Writing for the Web is not the same as writing for print because people read differently on the Web. One of the impediments to online reading is physical: it's harder to read on a screen than it is to read on paper. Even the best computer monitors are hopelessly fuzzy compared with the crisp images on a glossy magazine page, and the extra effort this requires from human eyes and brains slows readers down. The longer the document, the bigger the problem.

The physical impediment will lessen—and perhaps even disappear—in time. Today's monitors are vastly better than the ones in use a decade ago, especially the latest generation with flat screens and liquid crystal displays. Better software is also helping. Microsoft, for instance, has created a superior family of type fonts specifically designed for online reading (Arial and Tahoma are two of the most widely used). Innovation continues.

But the more significant barrier Web writers must overcome is behavioral, not physical, and technological advances may never break it down. Everyone who's observed, tested, or studied online reading agrees that people behave differently when online. When viewing a new page, they don't read—they scan. They look at headings and subheadings first; they scan for hyperlinks, numerals, and keywords. They jump around, scrolling and clicking, their fingers never far from the browser's "Back" button. The word that best describes their behavior is: impatient.

The challenge for the Web writer is to overcome readers' impatience by keeping things as brief as possible. It's a big challenge. Writing 250 breezy words on a given subject is usually harder than writing 1,000. The more experience you gain as a writer or editor, the more keenly you will understand what Blaise Pascal, the seventeenth-century French philosopher, meant when he apologized to a correspondent, "I have made this letter longer than usual, because I lack the time to make it shorter."

SHORTER IS BETTER

The key difference between writing for the Web and writing for offline readers is that Web writing needs to be shorter. Documents intended for online reading should rarely be longer than 1,000 words—a good target to aim for is 600–700. There are many approaches and devices that can help you learn to write more concisely, although an exhaustive review of them is beyond the scope of this guide. But we'll mention a few.

If it is possible to cut out a word, always cut it out

This profound rule for keeping your content short comes from the English novelist George Orwell, who also happened to be one of the masters of twentieth-century English (see ORWELL'S RULES in the A to Z). It is almost magical in its ability to streamline prose and expose rhetorical weakness.

Let's apply the rule to a newspaper article, picked at random from the January 7, 2001 *New York Times*. The first paragraph of the lead story read:

> Washington, Jan. 6—One thing is already clear about how President-elect George W. Bush intends to govern the nation: state and local officials will have far more leeway to shape and operate the full range of federal social, regulatory, and public works programs.

Applying Orwell's rule gives this:

> Washington, Jan. 6—One thing is clear about how George W. Bush intends to govern: state and local officials will have more leeway to shape and operate federal social, regulatory, and public works programs.

That takes the excerpt from 40 to 31 words—a 23 percent decrease without affecting its content.

This rule can be extended to cover phrases, sentences, and thoughts, as well as words. Once you've completed a draft of your content, read it again, asking yourself as you go along: "Is there superfluous information here?" and "Could these details be cut?"

A similar rule is embodied in William Faulkner's phrase "kill your darlings." Or as Samuel Johnson put it: "Read over your compositions, and wherever you meet with a passage which you think is particularly fine, strike it out." This sounds like suicidal advice but it makes a lot of sense. Often we fall in love with pet phrases or words. Subconsciously, we tend to write sentences that allow us to use them. This is not a good idea because it takes the writer away from the reason they sat down to write in the first place: to communicate something useful. Which brings us to a golden rule ...

Write for the reader, not for your ego

It's easy to just write and write, with no particular reader in mind. The problem with this sort of writing is that nobody reads it. Always keep the reader in mind. Think of them as busy, impatient people who are on the Web to find out something.

Question your modifiers

One of the characteristics of bad writing is its overuse of adjectives and adverbs. They add to the length of an article and also tend to slow its pace. When you look at them a second time, you often find they are disguising weak nouns and verbs. Think about the sentence, "He hit it really hard," then compare it with "He clobbered it."

BE DIRECT

"Begin at the beginning, and go on till you come to the end: then stop." Web readers would be eternally grateful if Web writers always followed that piece of advice (delivered by the King of Hearts to the White Rabbit in Lewis Carroll's *Alice's Adventures in Wonderland*).

But all too often, as any frustrated Web reader knows, writers do nothing of the kind. Instead of beginning an article about growing tomatoes with a clear statement telling you what you can expect to read (such as: "The best way to grow tomatoes is ... ") they will either begin with an anecdote ("It was a hot summer day when I first visited the sun-drenched fields of Sicily ... "), or with a barrage of information tangential to the main topic ("The soil in the Red River Valley of the north is known for its fertility—second, some of the locals say, only to the steppes of Russia ... "), or, perhaps most common on the Web, with personal superfluous information ("My name is John, I've been an amateur gardener for three years, and I created this page using Shovelworks for Imagemaker ... ").

Such indirect beginnings for articles are fine for certain kinds of writing. The anecdotal introduction, for instance, is a storyteller's staple and can be very effective. (Who could forget Hunter S. Thompson's beginning to *Fear and Loathing in Las Vegas*, first serialized in *Rolling Stone* magazine: "We were somewhere around Barstow on the edge of the desert when the drugs began to take hold.") But in most Web writing—especially business writing—the best way to begin is with the shortest and clearest statement you can make about your topic.

People on the Web are usually looking for information, and if you make it easy to find, they will thank you. If you bury what you actually want to communicate in the second or third paragraph, no one may read your article at all: research shows that Web readers scan pages before they read anything, meaning they may scan right past your article if it doesn't have a straightforward heading or introduction that includes key words about your topic.

Writers often opt for indirect introductions because of their insecurity. They fear that what they have to say will be so unexciting that potential readers will be turned off, so they try to find an indirect but more interesting way to draw the reader in. But doing this actually makes things worse. If you're writing about tomatoes, and the reader isn't interested in tomatoes, it's better to get it over with fast. Readers who've had to wade through several paragraphs before finding out they're in the wrong place will be all the more annoyed.

So be courageous when you sit down to write, and don't blame yourself if it takes a while to come up with an introduction that works. As anyone who's tried to write knows, beginning is often the most difficult part of the writing process. The blank sheet of paper is so anxiety-inducing that it's become a metaphor for writer's block. Writing for the Web is even worse: not only is the screen blank, but there in the upper-left-hand corner is the cursor, blinking away as if to mock your inability to get started.

WEB HEADINGS THAT WORK

On the Web, you live or die by your headings (or *headlines* as they are called in newspapers and magazines). A good one makes it easier for readers to find your article, and much more likely that they will read what you have written. A bad heading ensures that few, if any, readers will find your text at all, and that those who do will be unlikely to read further.

People don't begin to read your Web article by accident. First they have to find it. Potential readers will usually come to your article either from a crowded Webpage—where your article is just one of several clickable elements—or worse still, from a page full of search engine results. In either case, all the reader sees is the heading and the first sentence or so from the article (if they're lucky). If your heading doesn't grab them, you lose them—probably forever.

Writing headings for Web articles is a craft. Sometimes it almost seems to be an art. To learn from examples of heading writing at its best, look at top-quality advertising campaigns, front-page headlines in tabloid newspapers, and the cover lines of successful magazines. Madison Avenue's best advertising slogans succeed so well, they enter our common language. Think of Nike's "Just Do It" line.

Tabloid newspaper editors are among the best of all heading writers, since they know that nothing will do a better job of selling their papers than a short, compelling headline in big type. Two famous tabloid headlines: *The New York Daily News*, reporting on former US president Gerald Ford's decision to deny emergency funds to New York City during a fiscal squeeze:

FORD TO CITY:
DROP DEAD!

Or the *New York Post*'s account of a gruesome strip-club murder:

HEADLESS BODY
IN TOPLESS BAR

Magazine editors face a similar challenge. The would-be magazine buyer is looking at a rack of dozens or even hundreds of magazines, and will make a purchasing decision in minutes or seconds. The cover line is the first—and often the only—thing the potential buyer reads.

In 1998, a group of *Fortune* magazine editors spent 45 minutes debating the "cover line" for the magazine's annual retirement guide. They came up with a two-word headline that drove sales up an incredible 51 percent, making it the most popular issue in the magazine's 70-year history and increasing revenue by hundreds of thousands of dollars:

RETIRE RICH

These examples of winning headline writing share common attributes that are all applicable to the Web. Let's look at a couple of them here.

Headings should be short and direct

Remember that Web readers are usually looking for something, and the more efficiently you tell them what it is you've got, the better your heading will work. To be effective and attract the reader, headings should use "keywords." Studies have shown that people who use search engines predominantly type in 1–2 keywords for their search, rather than sentences or phrases. So, if you're writing about Microsoft's earnings, whatever else you do, use both words—"Microsoft" and "earnings"—in your heading!

Never try to be indirect and cute. Many writers and editors make this mistake, and write headings such as this, taken from a brokerage house report about technology stock prices:

Much Ado about Nothing

Erudite? Your call. Amusing? Only if you read the first section of the article, and then only mildly so. But such a heading guarantees that people looking for information about tech stock prices will never see the article. Try typing that heading into a search engine such as AltaVista. You'll get a million results, nearly all of them concerning drama and literature.

Use powerful language

Good headings share another attribute: nearly all have some kind of power in their language. Try not to undersell your content. If you're writing about the biggest something, say so! If profits have plunged, don't say they've decreased. Use the active rather than the passive voice, and try to use a strong verb—say "Ad agencies cut jobs," not "Layoffs announced by some agencies."

But don't deceive your reader either. If your article is about an incremental improvement in browser software, don't call it "The browser wars erupt again." Web readers are smart and unforgiving. The merest whiff of a bait-and-switch—promising one thing and then delivering another—sends them instantly to the Back button, and they'll stay away from your site forever.

USE SUBHEADS

One proven device for keeping a reader moving forward through an article is to insert subheads (subheadings) every few paragraphs. Just as a well-written heading can draw a reader into a story that they might otherwise skip over, subheads provide a visual road-sign, alerting readers that something different and potentially interesting is coming up.

The job of the subhead is to pick out a word, phrase, or idea from the following few paragraphs that will make the reader want to keep reading. The cleverest newspaper editors use a similar device when they have an article that is so long it must "jump" from one page to the next. Just before the article jumps, make sure there's an intriguing phrase. One feature-article editor for *The Wall Street Journal* used to say that the ultimate sentence that could appear before a "jump" was "... and then the shit hit the fan."

This approach is not unlike the classic "cliffhanger" that film and TV directors use to end an episode in a serial movie or TV show—the heroine dangling over a chasm, moments away from death. To find out what happens, you need to tune in again.

But subheads don't necessarily need to be dramatic. If you're writing a story about a stock-market analyst's predictions, for instance, and the analyst is saying that the overall market will decline over the next year but that stocks in a particular sector will rise, you'll need to lead with one idea or the other—probably the overall market. But a well-placed subheading that says "Companies that will buck the trend" will entice at least some readers to continue to that section.

Subheads not only keep articles moving along, they also serve a design function by breaking up the otherwise uniform blocks of type into less-forbidding looking chunks.

For subheads to be truly effective on the Web, they must be used liberally. Some websites use subheads but place them too far apart to be helpful. A subhead every six or seven paragraphs can be okay in print, but only because a reader is looking at a much larger piece of text than the Web reader ever sees at a given moment. The subheads used in this introduction, for instance, would be much too widely spaced for the Web. Online, either on the Web or in email, you should insert subheads often enough so that a reader never scrolls for more than a screen and a half without seeing one.

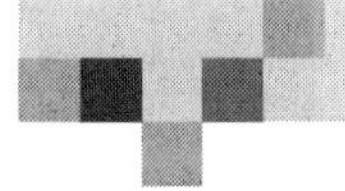

WEB PARAGRAPHS ARE DIFFERENT

To make your documents efficient and attractive for online readers, you need to ensure that the structure of the writing—the way that sentences and paragraphs are arranged on the screen—is suitable for Web reading. Among the most important elements of structure for online reading is paragraph length.

Although you can consult a dozen writing guides and find many "rules" about how to write paragraphs, there really aren't any rules. The ideal paragraph length depends not only on the kind of writing you're doing and the style and tone you adopt but also on the format and medium in which you're writing. It's as much a visual as a verbal issue.

Different kinds of writing demand different average paragraph lengths. The classic tabloid newspaper style is to make each sentence a paragraph, and to keep each sentence short. Paragraphs average fewer than a dozen words. This creates a telegraphic, immediate style appropriate for news stories, and is well suited to the narrow text columns of tabloids. "Quality" broadsheet newspapers favor a more discursive style. Paragraphs in the *New York Times*, for instance, tend to be more in the range of 50–60 words.

The structure for formal essays—followed by many magazine and book writers—runs toward longer paragraphs, sometimes considerably longer. This is the style of writing usually taught in schools. Ideally, each paragraph deals with a single thought. The first sentence is the "topic sentence," setting forth the main idea. The thought is developed in succeeding sentences. Distinctions and connections are made, qualifications are introduced, and examples given. Further points are sometimes included; contrasting material is sometimes provided as well.

This kind of formal paragraph can easily run on to 100 or more words, with no real upward limit. Some notable writers—Marcel Proust, for example—wrote paragraphs that go on for pages. At some point, however, the thought is concluded—typically with a short sentence.

The preceding four paragraphs of this article, in fact, would make up such a "classic" paragraph, and many book editors would have run them together into one paragraph. Altogether, they are 270 words. But even in a book like this, such a fat, dense paragraph could be off-putting. On a Webpage, it would be deadly. It would be like walking into a McDonald's and being ushered to a table with linen and silverware and a six-page menu. Not what you had in mind.

The rules for structuring writing for print have evolved over centuries; the rules for structuring online text are still emerging. In this, as in many other questions of online style, it's instructive to look at what the most successful websites do. Check out the way that sites like Yahoo, Excite, Microsoft, and CNET handle paragraph length.

As you'll see, on the Web—generally speaking—shorter is better. One of the handiest tools for the online writer is the word processor's word-count function. Try it. Live by it. If you're consistently writing paragraphs with more than 50 words, you should probably lighten up.

(The paragraph you've just read, at 47 words, is about the right length for the Web.)

KEEP YOUR SENTENCES SIMPLE

One of the best ways to make your writing Web friendly is to keep your sentences short and simple. Long, convoluted sentences, which may read very nicely in print (such as this one), will often seem forbidding on screen. They can distract your readers from their primary goal of finding information.

There are essentially three kinds of sentences, the first of which is the simple sentence. The simple sentence contains a verb, and usually a subject. It may or may not have an object. The famous first line of Herman Melville's *Moby Dick*, for instance, is: "Call me Ishmael." Another notable simple-sentence first line introduces Norman Mailer's *The Naked and the Dead*. It reads: "Nobody could sleep."

Second is the compound sentence, which is basically two simple sentences that are related. An example would be: "The Nasdaq crashed, and investors were devastated."

Finally comes the complex sentence, which includes a dependent clause. To embellish the last example, a typical complex sentence would be: "The Nasdaq crashed, and investors were devastated because they didn't see it coming." ("Because they didn't see it coming" is the dependent clause.)

From there, you can weave together compound and complex sentences until you have a very tangled Web indeed. Some novelists—Dostoyevsky, and Faulkner, for instance—are famous for writing extremely long sentences.

But the intent of most online writing is neither to dazzle the reader with literary technique nor to see how much you can cram into a single sentence; the intent is to communicate as quickly and efficiently as possible. This holds especially true for news and business writing.

Consider the following sentence, from a *New York Times* News Service dispatch posted on the *International Herald Tribune* site:

> The situation here, already tense, turned explosive earlier this month when the international administration, put in place after the 1995 peace accord that ended the war in Bosnia, ordered a raid on Herzegovacka Bank and nine of its branches.

By the end of the sentence the clauses are so entwined that it takes an effort to remember the main point. The sentence should probably have been rewritten entirely, but a quick fix would have been to excise the clause about the origin of the international administration and use it as a new, second sentence in parentheses. The passage would then read:

> The situation here, already tense, turned explosive earlier this month when the international administration ordered a raid on Herzegovacka Bank and nine of its branches. (The administration was put in place after the 1995 peace accord that ended the war in Bosnia.)

In addition to the three classic sentence types, there is the sentence fragment. Despite what some members of the literati teach, there's nothing wrong with using sentence fragments. Think of the ways they can be effective: For variety. For emphasis. Really!

A pedantic magazine editor once objected to a writer's use of sentence fragments in general, and of single-word sentences in particular. In the heat of the moment, the editor asked the writer: "Do you really think you can use single-word sentences whenever you feel like it?" To which the writer could think of only one reply: "Yes."

GETTING READY TO WRITE

One of the simple tricks that professional writers learn can greatly ease the process of getting ready to write: look for a model of the kind of article you need to do, then dissect it, analyze it—and copy it. Beginners sometimes worry that this is cheating, if not plagiarism, but it's nothing of the kind. It is, indeed, the way novice writers were traditionally trained at newspapers and wire services. (PLAGIARISM, though, is a subject of increasing importance on the Web, and is dealt with in the A to Z index.)

For aspiring Web writers, this means becoming familiar with the best websites that feature the kinds of articles that you're seeking to write. In addition to content formats, you will also see the best-practice approach to writing headings and summaries.

If you're writing a corporate news bulletin, for instance, you could do a lot worse than visit one of the top news sites, such as "TECH NEWS" at ZDNet (www.zdnet.com) and see how their stories are constructed. Here's the heading and first three paragraphs of an article that appeared on April 2, 2001:

NETCENTIVES TO CUT 120 JOBS

U.S. Web-based marketing firm Netcentives said on Monday it would cut about 120 jobs in a cost-cutting effort that would help bring its earnings per share above Wall Street's forecasts.

In a statement, Netcentives also said President Eric Larsen would become chief executive, replacing West Shell III. Shell will remain chairman.

Netcentives said a cost-cutting effort would save about $40 million in the 2001 fiscal year. "The company's cost reduction plan includes several initiatives such as: a reduction in contract labor; cuts in administrative, travel and capital expenditures; and a reduction in work force of approximately 120 people," the statement said.

The heading is short, to the point, and factual. The first paragraph gives just a bit of background about the company, states the news, and tells you "why" the company says it's doing what it's doing. The second paragraph gives the next-most-important news. The third fills out the news a bit, and provides a direct quote from the company's press release.

That's a pretty good recipe for a breaking-news story, and a novice writer trying to put together a news piece could save a lot of potential flailing around by adopting the format.

Say you're asked to write a fact sheet for a corporation. A good place to start would be at one of the slicker Fortune 500 company websites, such as General Electric's, and see what they do. At www.ge.com/factsheet.html you'll find a two-page fact sheet that's an excellent model.

GE's fact sheet begins with a tight two-paragraph "About GE" section, then has a complete "financial highlights" section, and a listing of awards and honors the company has received. The second page features 20 one-paragraph descriptions of GE's business segments (linked to the appropriate parts of the website) and, finally, a social responsibility statement.

Although the company you're describing won't warrant the exact same treatment (few companies have as many business segments as GE!), this fact sheet is an excellent model of Web-friendly writing and design.

Novice writers often make two mistakes: they think they need to be entirely original, and they think they need to wait for "inspiration." Take it from the pros: for most kinds of writing, originality and inspiration are overrated. There are only a few ways to begin an article, and most often, the right one won't seem very original. As for inspiration, writers should always bear in mind that old maxim of Thomas Alva Edison: "Genius is 1 percent inspiration and 99 percent perspiration."

When getting ready to write, always try to read the type of writing your reader reads. Say your target reader is a financial analyst, chances are they'll read the *Wall Street Journal* and the *Financial Times*. Read a number of issues. If nothing else, you'll get a feel for the basic tone and style of financial writing. For the writer who wants to get published, read the content your target editor publishes. It will give you a sense of what kind of writing to emulate.

EDITING YOURSELF

Learning to write polished, concise prose is a difficult, sometimes maddening process. Learning how to do it routinely, under deadline pressure, is exceedingly difficult. The authors of this book have been at it, professionally, for a collective 40 years, and are still learning.

There are, however, some simple techniques—tricks, you could say—that can help any aspiring writer become more effective. One of these tricks is more about mindset than mechanics: force yourself to switch roles, think like an editor, and critique your own writing. This can bring new discipline to the writing process.

For many writers, getting the first rough draft of a memo, report, or article onto the screen is the most laborious and painful part of the writing process: organizing your ideas, wresting them from your mind into words and phrases, sentences and paragraphs, confronting the fact that what you have to say rarely seems as good on the screen as it did in your thoughts—none of it is easy. This is probably what Samuel Johnson was thinking when he noted that "No man but a blockhead ever wrote ... except for money."

No wonder, then, that most writers—and nearly all novices—are only too willing to wash their hands of their first draft as soon as they've finally got it all down. But what the best professional writers learn is that they can improve their writing significantly if they can switch roles at this point, take a break, then return to their writing, but this time looking at it from the point of view of an editor. Again, your word processor's word-count function is an invaluable tool: count the number of words you've written, and set an objective for cutting them back. Many experienced writers routinely cut their own first drafts by anywhere from 25 percent to 50 percent.

The editor's motivations are very different from a writer's. The editor must be an advocate for the reader, not for the writer. Uppermost in the editor's mind is the question of how easily the reader will be able to grasp what the writer is trying to say. The editor isn't concerned—at least not primarily—with how difficult it was for the writer to write the article, how proud the writer is of a particular word or phrase, how hard the writer worked to shoehorn a particular fact or anecdote or detail into the article.

The editor must question every word and every sentence, asking

- Is this clear?
- Is there a simpler way to say this?
- Is there a shorter way to say this?
- Is this necessary?

The editor must be willing to rephrase anything that's ambiguous, to simplify anything that's unnecessarily complex, and to cut whatever isn't essential—to cut entire sentences or paragraphs, if needs be.

The first trick in editing yourself is to leave enough time. If you're writing a 500-word article and it's due Friday morning, make sure you finish it Thursday morning so that you can set it aside for a few hours, go have lunch, then return to it, prepared to devote another couple of hours to it.

The second and harder trick is to put yourself into the mindset of an editor. One way to do this is to make a game of it. Pretend that someone else has written the piece and that it's your job to expose its weaknesses. Talk to yourself about the writer. Say, "Okay, what is he trying to do here?" Better yet, say things like, "What was she thinking here?" and "Do we really need this last paragraph?" The object is to detach yourself from the ego that the writer—you—has invested in the article.

Some writers find that a good way to critique their own work is to print it out at this point, and make corrections, changes, and queries in pen or pencil on the written draft. Switching media somehow seems to aid the process of viewing a piece of writing objectively. Then take the marked-up copy and go back and rewrite what you have on the screen.

Try it, and as an experiment, keep a copy of both your first draft and your final self-edited draft. After a week or two, go back and compare the two. Chances are, this exercise will make a believer of you.

A FINAL THOUGHT

People have been writing, editing, and publishing for millennia. The best minds of human civilization have thought long and hard about the optimal techniques for communicating in print. Much of that accumulated wisdom has held true as the technology of publishing has changed, from clay tablets to papyrus scrolls to bound books, newspapers and magazines, and to the World Wide Web today. It's silly to throw it all away, and many of the rules and suggestions in this book build directly on that knowledge. But at the same time, you must be ever-mindful of what is truly unique about the Web. This book attempts to identify those differences, and present them in a format that can serve as a handy everyday reference for anyone who writes or edits content online.

DESIGNING FOR THE WEB II

In the early days of the Web, the creators of websites were primarily techies. They tended to have quantitative rather than verbal skills; they had studied languages such as C++ rather than English; they were the kids in college who hung out in the computer labs rather than at the student newspaper. In short, they didn't have a lot of experience with publications.

Many early Web-heads were at pains to emphasize the differences between the Web and printed media, and were thus hostile to any rules or standards that appeared to be print-based. And when they did import skilled people from print media, it tended to be graphic artists. As anyone who's worked in the print world can tell you, graphic artists are very concerned with art, but are not always too worried about whether the type on the page is readable.

But Web design is about content design, it's about laying out content so that it can be read easily. It's about organizing content so that it can be navigated and searched with ease. It's about getting the right content to the right reader at the right time. For the majority of websites, what Web design is *not* is graphic or visually driven design. To design for the Web, you need to understand what the Web actually is, rather than what some would like it to be. The Web is a place people come to find stuff (content). It's a functional place. Most people don't hang around on the Web. They come to the Web to do things. Study after study reinforces the practical, functional mindset of the person who comes to the Web.

What's the number one thing people do on the Web? They *read*. Words and numbers are the raw material from which the vast majority of Webpages are built. If reading is the primary activity on the Web, then readability is a primary function of Web design. Another primary activity on the Web is search and navigation. It follows, therefore, that the organization of content to make it easily searchable and navigable is a primary function of Web design.

The number one design principle for the Web is simplicity. Quality Web design should be all about making life easier for the reader to find content, and then making it easy for them to read that content.

DESIGN FOR THE READER

Remember, your website is a publication and the people who come to it are readers. Therefore the first step in the design of any website is understanding who your reader is. Who is it that might come to your website? What content will they want if they do come? What are they going to read?

To design a great website, you also need to understand the characteristics of the online reader. They

- gather content—they know broadly what they are looking for but not exactly
- scan read—they are practical, impatient, in a hurry
- are skeptical and suspicious—they know there's an awful lot of junk on the Web
- are conservative—once they find a website they like, they'll stick with it

Any design must make sure that it is as easy as possible to read (black text on white background, sans serif fonts, reasonable font sizes, and so on). In addition, because people scan read, the presentation and layout of the content needs to facilitate such an activity (punchy headings, summaries, short paragraphs).

EVERY WEBSITE IS A DIRECTORY

Why did Amazon.com choose books as its first product offering? A key reason was that there was already a sophisticated electronic directory of published books that Amazon could plug into. Amazon may have lots of interesting services, but without its directories, it would be like a shop without shelves (see Figure 2.1).

FIGURE 2.1

The Amazon homepage is all about giving attention. Everything is oriented around selling things to the consumer. The logo, as is the web convention, is small and is located in the top left corner.

Why were so many people excited about Yahoo when it started? Because it launched a directory. Before Yahoo, it was very hard to know what was on the Web. Yahoo may have added a lot of services over the years, but its foundation is still a directory of quality websites (see Figure 2.2).

Why was eBay so successful? Because it created a directory for people who wanted to buy and sell second-hand stuff. Without proper classification, eBay would have quickly descended into chaos as it grew. But because its growth was based on a comprehensive classification system, it works.

FIGURE 2.2

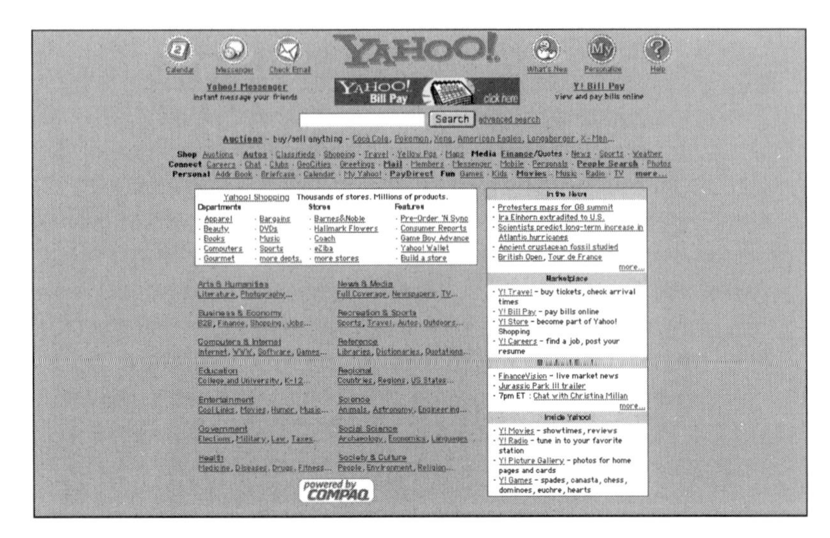

Yahoo still behaves fundamentally as a directory that helps people quickly find the content they are looking for.

Napster became a hugely successful brand. How did Napster build its brand? By providing people with an efficient way to find and download the music they want. Graphically, the Napster website does not look very sophisticated. Its logo looks like it was designed on the back of a beer mat. But its power, like all the best websites, is under the surface. Its power is not in how it looks but in how it works.

The Web is all about publishing content in an organized manner. All the great websites are driven by great directories that allow people to quickly find the content they want. Those websites that fail are those that frustrate the reader. They don't classify their content well. Their search doesn't work well. Their navigation is poor. Their pages are full of big graphics that take ages to download.

Great Web design must be founded on great directory (classification) design. Anybody who wants to design for the Web must understand how to create professional classifications. They need to know how to design an efficient search process, and how to create a navigation design for a website that is as intuitive as possible.

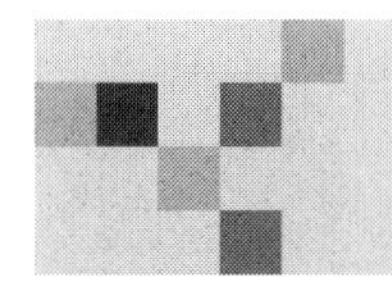

FROM GETTING ATTENTION TO GIVING ATTENTION

What makes a website great is what is below the surface, not what is above. Too many Web designers focus on the shiny stuff—the fancy graphics, the clever animations. Study after study shows that people are just not interested in this surface sheen. In fact, in many cases this visual-driven design gets in the way of people doing what they want to do.

Many marketers and advertisers are still struggling to come to terms with the Web. They are bringing old thinking and old skills to a new medium. It's true that in an attention-deficit economy, the job of the marketer is very often to get attention for the brand. They constantly need to make their brand stand out in a global traffic jam of brands.

However, how does someone get to a website? By either clicking a link or typing in a website address. First, they have done something active. Second, they are aware of where they want to go. It's to ibm.com, microsoft.com, ebay.com, yahoo.com, napster.com.

What's common to all these websites addresses? Brands! When someone comes to your website, you have *already got* their attention. The job of the website is to *give* attention. The person has come to the website with a need. They should leave the website with that need fulfilled.

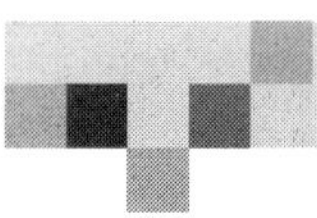

STRUCTURE IS BORING, BUT IT WORKS

Website design can be boring and monotonous, because for all its revolutionary potential, the Web is a very functional place. Classification (directory) design is the science of organizing large quantities of content in an efficient and intuitive manner so that people can find what they're looking for quickly. Directories will always have some sort of A to Z classification structure. There's nothing wrong with that. People don't say: "I wish they'd do something other than an A to Z for a change. Maybe Z to A, or A to L, followed by Z to M."

The reason that people will never get bored with an A to Z directory design is the same reason they never get bored with street sign design. You don't hear tourists complaining that the street signs in such-and-such a country are all the same design. That's because the tourist is not there to visit the signs; they're there to visit the places on the signs. It's the same with classification. The classification system is not what interests the reader; it's the content that the classification holds that's of interest.

People see the Web as a single huge place. What they learn through navigating around one website, they like to bring with them to another website. Take hypertext, for example. The original design for hypertext was blue for unclicked and purple for clicked. People like it because they're used to it. So when they see a blue link, they know that's a part of the website they haven't been to. When they see a purple link, they know that's a part of the website they have visited. Changing the color of the hyperlinks just confuses people. It's like having red and green traffic signals in one part of town, and orange and yellow in another.

THE WEB IS ALSO LIKE A NEWSPAPER

It's not enough to have a great directory of content for your website. There's another key publishing skill that you require. It recognizes the fact that most of the time we don't know exactly what content we want when we come to a website. A study by Xerox Park found that 75 percent of Web readers are in "content-gathering" mode, with only 25 percent having a specific document or file that they want to find.

When people come to your website, almost 8 out of 10 of them are saying: "Okay, you've got my attention. Now, tell me something interesting. Any special offers? Any new products? New features? Inform me. Educate me. Give me guidance." This is what newspapers do well. They organize the best and most important content and present it to people in a highly readable format.

The best way to explain this newspaper or editorial-based approach is through an example. Say you have a problem with the software for your Iomega zip drive. You go to the company's website and search for replacement software under the model name "zip 250." You will quickly find the page with the appropriate software, which is free. But beside it is a description of another piece of software that does something special (see Figure 2.3).

FIGURE 2.3

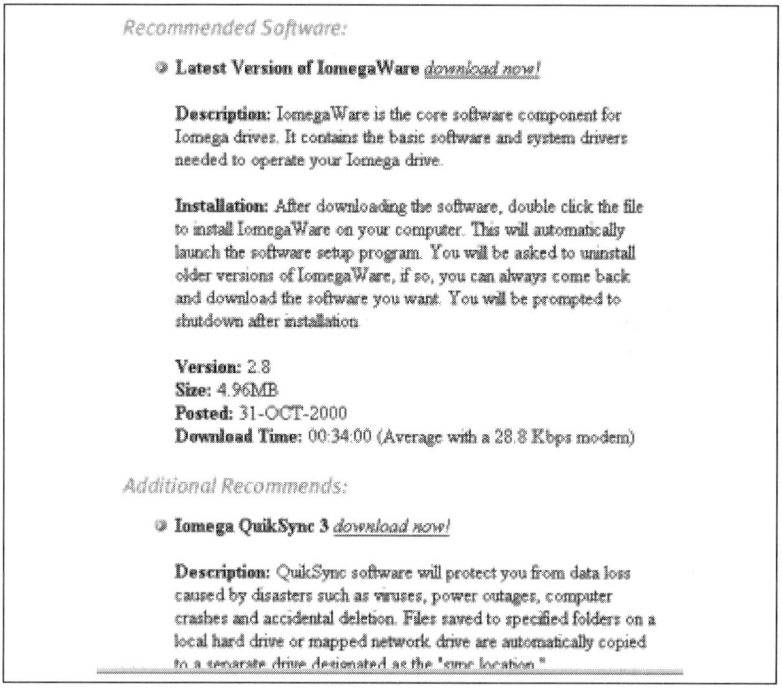

Recommended Software:

Latest Version of IomegaWare *download now!*

Description: IomegaWare is the core software component for Iomega drives. It contains the basic software and system drivers needed to operate your Iomega drive.

Installation: After downloading the software, double click the file to install IomegaWare on your computer. This will automatically launch the software setup program. You will be asked to uninstall older versions of IomegaWare, if so, you can always come back and download the software you want. You will be prompted to shutdown after installation.

Version: 2.8
Size: 4.96MB
Posted: 31-OCT-2000
Download Time: 00:34:00 (Average with a 28.8 Kbps modem)

Additional Recommends:

Iomega QuikSync 3 *download now!*

Description: QuikSync software will protect you from data loss caused by disasters such as viruses, power outages, computer crashes and accidental deletion. Files saved to specified folders on a local hard drive or mapped network drive are automatically copied to a separate drive designated as the "sync location."

Iomega recommends IomegaWare software for its Zip 250 product. However, it also recommends QuikSync 3, which has additional features. This is what ecommerce is: selling with content.

One reason you have a zip drive may be because you need to back up your files regularly in case your computer goes awry or gets damaged. This special software allows you to point a folder on your computer's hard drive to the backup disk on your zip drive. Having done that, every time you change a file within that folder on your hard drive, it will be backed up immediately. (How do you find that out? You read it.)

The software you came looking for is free. This special software costs $40. But you may well pay the $40 willingly. You didn't even know that this special software existed before you came to the website. But now that you've *read* about what extra benefits it can bring you, you'll seriously consider purchasing it.

This is newspaper-thinking design. It's about laying out content in the right place to catch the reader's attention just at the right time. It's about headings and summaries—short, snappy pieces of content placed in the right context.

This is what Web selling and marketing is about. On the Web you are selling your organization and products with your content. A newspaper will use a big picture of a plane crash and a screaming headline to grab attention. The Microsoft or Oracle website will lead with breezy content on new product releases, customer case studies, special offers. Their websites are designed in such a way that they can constantly update content that is fresh, engaging, and calls to the reader to click for more. It's like *Microsoft Daily* or *The Oracle Times*.

WEB LAYOUT IS SIMPLE LAYOUT

Newspaper design takes a uniform approach to layout because newspapers have found that there are only a few ways to lay out content for maximum readability. For starters, there are only two basic newspaper sizes: broadsheet and tabloid. If we were to lay out the front pages of 10 of the world's biggest-selling broadsheet newspapers in a row, they would be almost identical from a layout point of view. There would be a masthead, a lead story, several smaller stories, a large picture, some features running across the top, and perhaps an ad near the bottom (see Figure 2.4).

The Web is an even more limited design environment. It's harder to read from a screen than from paper. The average screen page is much smaller than a newspaper page. In theory, you can have audio, video, and animation, but bandwidth restrictions severely limit these multimedia options. Within this limited layout environment, a small number of layout conventions are emerging.

Those of you who were around at the beginning of the Web will have noticed a strange thing. You were told that the Web would change everything and that the Web was constantly changing. But as the years have

FIGURE 2.4

The Guardian

Israel gives up on peace with Sharon victory

THE TIMES

Russell 'killer' may be freed

THE SCOTSMAN

Teachers say yes to McCrone

THE IRISH TIMES

What makes newspapers different is not their layout but the stories they cover and how they write about these stories. The layout—as we can see from the four front pages—is almost identical. The difference is in the content. This should also apply to a website.

passed, the Web has become increasingly the same from a design and layout point of view.

Take background design. As the Web went through its first flush of youth, background design tended to look like sixties' psychedelia. Text sat on every color and "wallpaper" under the sun. White text on a black background was a favorite of the art school. Branding experts felt that their logos should be embossed on every page. You had green text to give an environmentalist feel. Red text in the middle of a paragraph gave emphasis. If the website sold cars you read gray text on a blue steering wheel background. It was great stuff—not!

All this experimentation might have been fun for the designer, but it was hell for the reader. The reality is that the eye finds it easiest to read black text on a white background. Small quantities of text are okay with different designs, but if you want someone to read more than 300 words, give it to them black on white. The Web pioneers learned that lesson—today, the vast majority of websites use black (or dark) type on white (or light) background (see Figure 2.5).

FIGURE 2.5

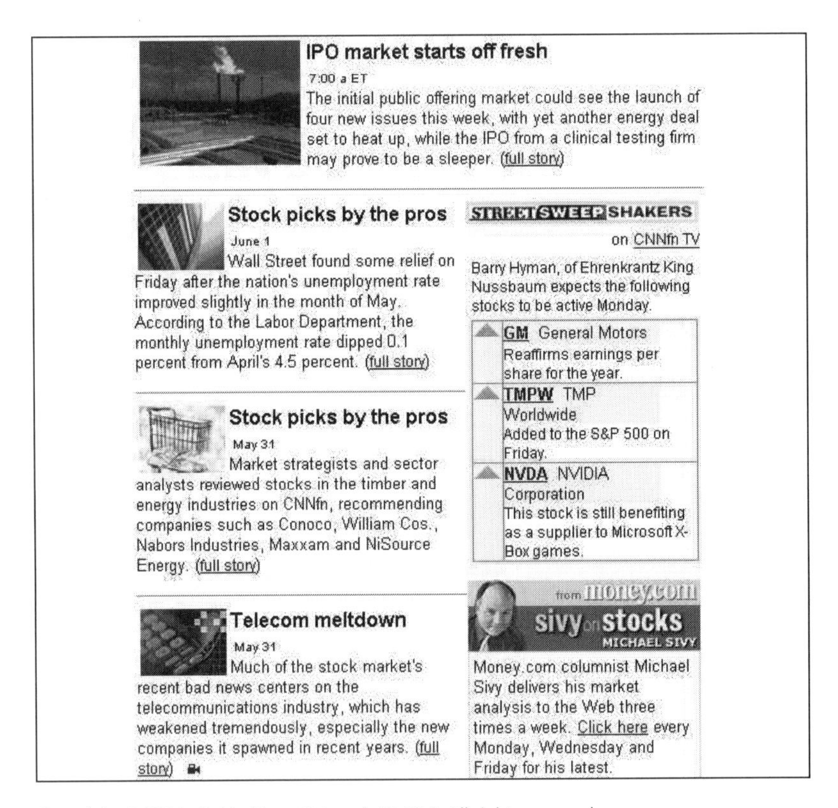

IPO market starts off fresh

7:00 a ET

The initial public offering market could see the launch of four new issues this week, with yet another energy deal set to heat up, while the IPO from a clinical testing firm may prove to be a sleeper. (full story)

Stock picks by the pros

June 1

Wall Street found some relief on Friday after the nation's unemployment rate improved slightly in the month of May. According to the Labor Department, the monthly unemployment rate dipped 0.1 percent from April's 4.5 percent. (full story)

Stock picks by the pros

May 31

Market strategists and sector analysts reviewed stocks in the timber and energy industries on CNNfn, recommending companies such as Conoco, William Cos., Nabors Industries, Maxxam and NiSource Energy. (full story)

Telecom meltdown

May 31

Much of the stock market's recent bad news centers on the telecommunications industry, which has weakened tremendously, especially the new companies it spawned in recent years. (full story)

STREETSWEEP SHAKERS

on CNNfn TV

Barry Hyman, of Ehrenkrantz King Nussbaum expects the following stocks to be active Monday.

GM General Motors
Reaffirms earnings per share for the year.

TMPW TMP Worldwide
Added to the S&P 500 on Friday.

NVDA NVIDIA Corporation
This stock is still benefiting as a supplier to Microsoft X-Box games.

from money.com
sivy on stocks
MICHAEL SIVY

Money.com columnist Michael Sivy delivers his market analysis to the Web three times a week. Click here every Monday, Wednesday and Friday for his latest.

This is a CNN page. Black text on a white background. Bold headings to draw attention. This page is easy to read.

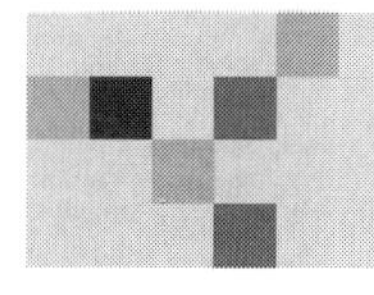

WEB DESIGN IS CONVENTIONAL DESIGN

The fact that newspapers use a uniform layout approach does not make them the same. Where text-based content is concerned, the style, uniqueness, and value is in the words, not in any graphics that surround the words. This is not to say that graphics have no role on the Web. They have, but it's very much a supporting role. They should enhance the presentation of content, and support the navigation through that content.

Like newspaper design and layout, the Web is evolving a uniform style for design and layout. Here is a sample of the Web design conventions that are emerging:

- Global navigation: This relates to a small selection of essential links that are presented on every page. This global navigation begins with a link to "Home."
- Masthead: This is the top-of-page area. It contains a logo on the left and a search box on the right or on the left, directly underneath the logo. Mastheads are getting very slim to maximize the amount of space for the presentation of content.
- Three-column layout: Designers have found that the optimal way to lay out the maximum quantity of content and navigation with the maximum readability is the three-column approach. The left column contains navigation, the middle recent content, the right features (see Figure 2.6).
- Footer: Every page should have a footer containing global navigation, contact details, copyright, and privacy links.

Implementing the above design conventions is in no way a cop-out. There is an old saying that geniuses steal, beggars borrow. The above conventions have been found to work. Readers won't look at your website and say, "ah, this is boring." Rather, they'll react by feeling comfortable, feeling familiar, feeling that they know how to navigate quickly.

FIGURE 2.6

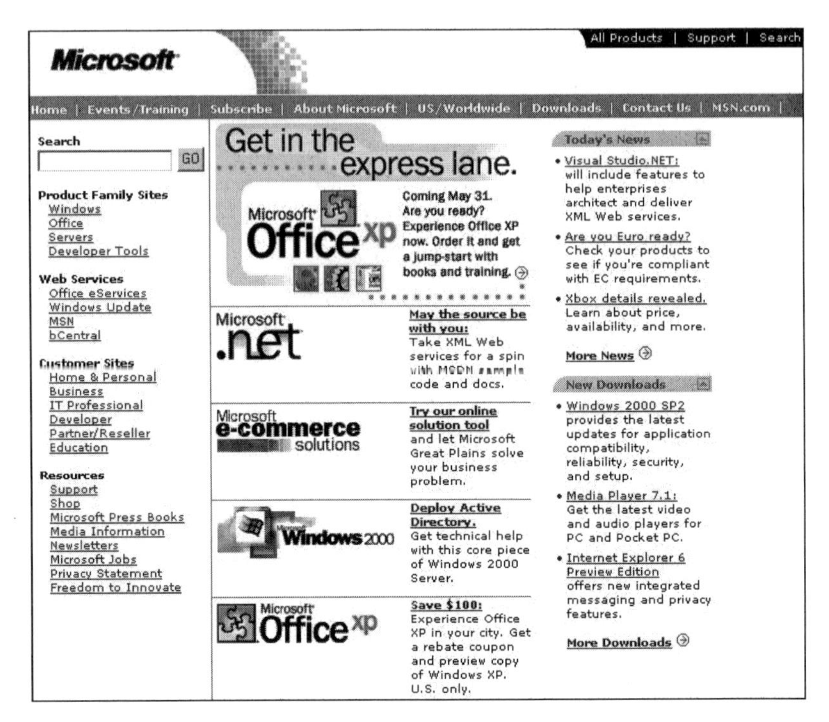

Microsoft.com is an example of a website that has a slim masthead, and a global navigation that begins with a "Home" link. The search is placed underneath the logo, and the rest of the page employs a three-column layout approach.

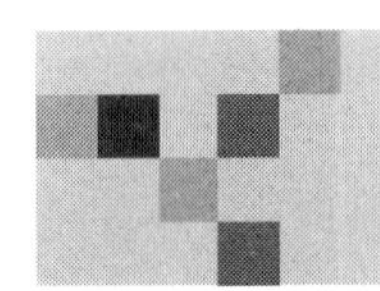

NAVIGATION AND SEARCH ARE CRITICAL

There are 550 billion documents on the Web—information overload in the extreme. When was the last time you went beyond the second page of a set of search results (even though there were 100,000 returned)? Your reader does not want to spend a long time looking for content on your website. If they don't see a result quickly, they're off to your competitor.

There are lots of complex-sounding words for organizing content on the Web: metadata, classification, taxonomy, XML, navigation. Take metadata, for example. Metadata may sound strange, but without it your website is like that proverbial needle in the haystack.

Metadata is the "who, what, where, when, and how" of a particular website. Think about it as an extension of grammar. Metadata is about classifying your content in a directory structure that will help the reader navigate to it easily. Metadata also collects keywords and other information on your content such as author name and date of publication. This sort of information makes the search of your website much more efficient. Without quality metadata, you are lost on the Web.

Metadata makes it possible to create quality navigation and search, which are the foundations on which all quality websites are built. Navigation deals with how readers move through a website, search is how readers search for something specific. The larger the website gets, the more critical navigation and search become. This is where the complexity and elegance of Web design come into play.

Navigation design is about providing a variety of logical paths through the content, such as allowing the reader to navigate by geographic sector or by subject matter (see Figure 2.7). It's about letting the reader know where they are (by using prominent section headings), where they've been (by using correctly colored hyperlinks), and where they're going (by using self-explanatory classification names) at all times.

It's about providing context for the reader—a classification issue that involves, for example, classifying all content on notebook computer X in the same section.

Navigation is about following Web convention—going with what the reader is familiar with—such as having the "Home" link as the first link on your global navigation running across every page on the site.

Designing a quality search is about making sure that you have quality metadata for every webpage so that search can be at its most efficient. It's also about having a search box on every page of your website. Remember, search is something that we do all the time. Don't hide your search behind a link (see Figure 2.6).

FIGURE 2.7

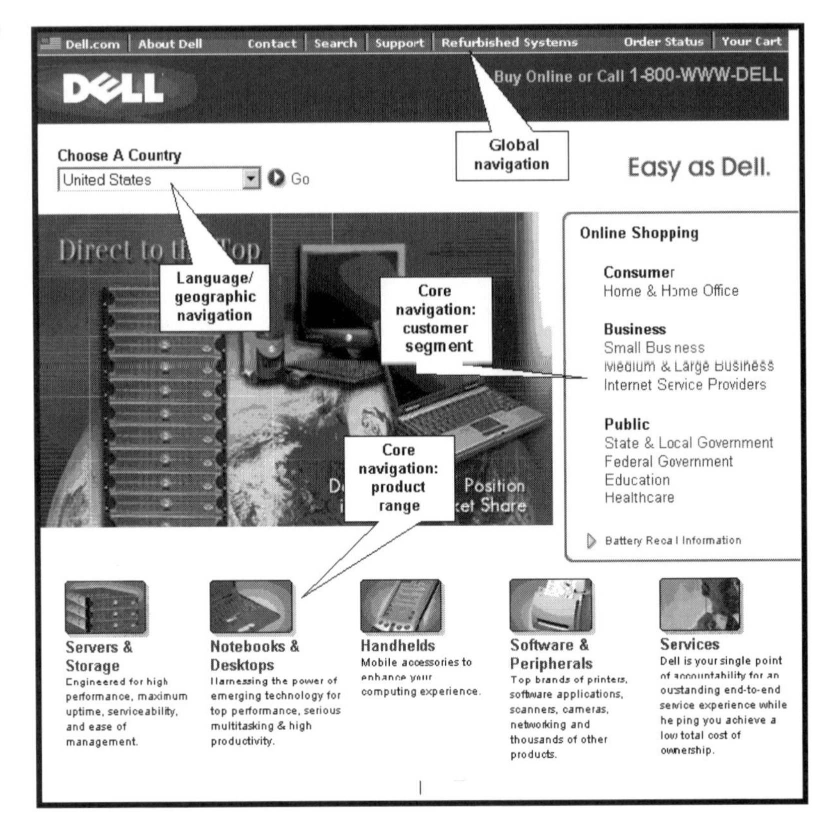

The Dell homepage is all about offering a variety of navigation options that help a potential customer to find the product they want the way they want.

DESIGN FOR INTERACTIVITY

When a reader comes to your website, you want them to do something positive, such as purchase your product. Surprise, surprise, the reader has the very same intention. Most of us don't go to the Web for the fun of it. We're action-oriented. We want to *do* something.

If you want to sell something, put it on the homepage. Never put up splash pages or anything else that might get in the way of the reader doing what they want to do. Keep your pages light and zippy so that they download quickly, because if they take longer than 10 seconds to download, most of your customers will be gone.

The Web is an interactive place, right? How many websites hide their contact details? Isn't it unbelievable that when you're looking for a telephone number, email, or postal address you can't find it?

Some readers want to voice their opinion, contribute to a discussion, join an online community. This interaction should be encouraged, but it also should be moderated. Discussion areas that are unmoderated quickly become disaster zones.

The Web is a "pull" medium. Every day you've got to bring readers back. That's no easy task. What you need are some "push" tools. An email newsletter is a great way of keeping your readers informed of what's happening. It should be a primary objective of every website to get people to subscribe to an email mail shot or newsletter. But make sure you send them only quality content and that you do it on a regular basis.

Talking of subscribing, people are paranoid about their privacy on the Web—and with good reason. If you are collecting information about people for subscription services or personalization, make sure you look after it, and don't abuse it. You'll lose customers if you do.

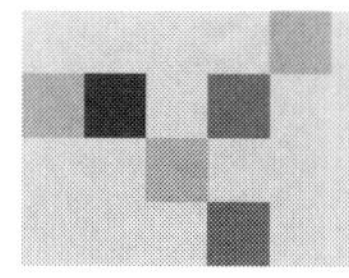

WEB DESIGN: KEEP IT SIMPLE, STRUCTURED, AND READER-CENTRIC

The Web was invented as a communications medium for publishing content. Publishing content on the Web is just like publishing content anywhere else. It needs to be concise, well written, well organized, well presented, and well targeted.

When designing a website, keep the following in mind:

- Design for the reader: If you don't have content that other people want, then you don't really have a reason to be on the Web.

- Make sure that your content is well organized, so that it is easy to search and navigate through.
- Lay out your homepage as if you were running a newspaper. Present short, exciting content that delivers a call to action to the reader.
- Follow Web convention: Don't be original in your layout; be original in your content.
- Design for interactivity: Where appropriate, encourage the reader to contribute, to give feedback.
- Keep it simple: A website should be so simple that even an adult can understand how to use it.

AN A TO Z OF WEB CONTENT STYLE

III

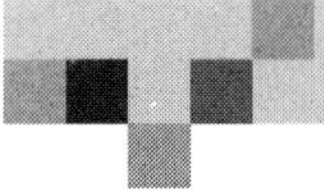

A

abbreviations and acronyms

Acronyms are abbreviations that form words from the first letter or letters in a series of words. For example, DOS is an acronym (as well as an abbreviation), while CPU is an abbreviation only as it does not form a word.

Abbreviations that are formed by using the first initials of separate words should not have any periods after the letters:

WAN, US, UK, PDF

Make an acronym or abbreviation plural by adding an *s* (no apostrophe), for example

WANs, PDAs

The article (*a* or *an*) that an abbreviation or acronym takes depends on the way it is pronounced—*an* if it's before a vowel sound, *a* before a consonant sound

an IBM computer
an FTP program (pronounced with a vowel sound)
a DOS command
a UN resolution (although UN starts with a vowel, it is not pronounced with a vowel sound—*you en*)

Generally, spell out unfamiliar abbreviations and acronyms at first mention, with the abbreviation immediately following in brackets, for example

Artificial intelligence (AI)

Thereafter, use the abbreviation only.

See also ARTICLES, CONTRACTIONS.

access devices

Any device used to access the Internet, including PCs, wireless devices, television, and public kiosks.

accessibility

Accessibility covers how easily a website can be used by people with disabilities. Although adherence to certain accessibility standards is demanded by law in an increasing number of countries, accessibility is not just about the law, it makes good sense from a design point of view. Making a website fully accessible generally improves the usability of the website for everyone involved.

It is often not practical to have your website meet every single accessibility standard. You should prioritize them and aim to make at least the homepage and other highly trafficked pages accessible. There are a number of organizations that provide detailed accessibility standards—probably the most notable are the W3C guidelines on Web Content Accessibility (www.w3.org/TR/WCAG10/), and the Electronic and Information Technology Accessibility Standards of the US Architectural And Transportation Barriers Compliance Board (www.access-board.gov/sec508/508standards.htm). Below, we have outlined the major points to consider.

- **Proper use of HTML**: If you use HTML the way it was intended, you will go a long way toward making your website accessible, since this allows alternative browsers to present the page in a way that is optimized for the reader. For example, don't use a header tag to change the font size. Also, ensure your documents are clear and simple and create a style of presentation that is consistent across pages. See also CSS.

- **Images:** Provide a text equivalent (normally ALT text) for all images to aid readers who cannot see the images. Ensure only client-side image maps are used. See ALT TEXT, GRAPHICS, IMAGE MAP, CLIENT SIDE.
- **Design:** The foreground and background color combinations should provide sufficient contrast. Avoid tiled backgrounds as they can obscure text. Ensure that all information conveyed with color is also available without color. See also COLOR.
- **Navigation:** Use navigation mechanisms in a consistent manner. Make links self-explanatory. Add metadata, general information about the layout of the site, and navigation bars. Use a consistent layout. Do not cause pop-ups or other windows to appear and do not change the current window without informing the reader. See also NAVIGATION.
- **Screen movement:** Try to avoid too much movement on the screen, including flickering screens or "blinking" content. Avoid creating auto-refresh pages. See also ANIMATION.
- **Technologies:** Avoid using non-standard technologies that require viewing with either plug-ins or stand-alone applications. When inaccessible technologies must be used, provide equivalent accessible pages if possible. See also FORMATS.
- **Tables:** Mark up tables correctly and clearly identify row and column headers. For data tables that have two or more logical levels of row or column headers, use mark up to associate data cells and header cells. Tables of any nature can present problems for users of screen readers. Do not use tables for layout unless the table makes sense when linearized. If a table is used for layout, do not use any structural markup for visual formatting. Preferably, use style sheets for layout and positioning.
- **Applets and scripts:** Ensure that pages can still be used even if they are viewed with a browser that does not support scripts, applets, or other programmatic objects. Ensure direct accessibility of embedded user interfaces. Design for device independence.
- **Frames:** Not recommended. However, if you must use them, ensure each frame is titled in order to facilitate navigation and frame identification. See also FRAMES.
- **Multimedia:** Provide an auditory description of the important

information of the visual track of a multimedia presentation. See also MULTIMEDIA.

- **Forms:** When forms are designed to be filled out online, allow people using assistive technology to access all the information, field elements, and functionality required for completion and submission of the form, including all directions and cues. See also FORMS.

address, physical

Always include your physical address on the website, preferably in the footer of every page. This reassures the reader that there's a "real" organization behind the site, as well as providing them with necessary information. If you have more than one address, you can keep the list behind a "contact" link. See also FOOTER.

address, Web

See WEB ADDRESS.

ADSL

Stands for asymmetric digital subscriber line, a specific type of high-speed digital subscriber line that offers download speeds of up to 9 megabits per second (Mbps) and upload speeds of up to 800 kilobits per second (Kbps).

advanced search

See SEARCH.

advertising

See PROMOTING CONTENT, BANNER AD.

advertorial

Advertiser-sponsored content that resembles editorial content and therefore contains a more "subtle" sell for that advertiser's products. Advertorials should be clearly marked as such. For example, "This article is sponsored by X" or "Advertisement." Readers have become quite cynical when using the Web, and if they feel that you're trying to pull a fast one on them, they will quickly reach for the Back button.

affect/effect

This is one of the most common mistakes in English. The verb *affect* means to influence. Do not confuse it with the verb *effect*, which means to cause. The noun *effect* is used more often and means result.

Sales were *affected* by the downturn in the economy. [Here, *affect* means the downturn *influenced* the sales figures.]

Sales were *effected* by the downturn in the economy. [In this case, used incorrectly, it means the downturn *caused* sales.]

The *effect* of the downturn in the economy on sales was disastrous. [Here, *effect* as a noun means "the result" as in the downturn *resulted* in fewer sales.]

afterward/afterwards

Afterward in American English, *afterwards* in British English.

ages/periods of history

Many names applied to historical or cultural periods are capitalized, particularly those recognized by archaeologists and anthropologists, for example

Bronze Age, Stone Age, the Renaissance

More general period designations are not capitalized, such as "golden age" and "fin de siècle." For more information, consult a stylebook such as *The Chicago Manual of Style*. As always, the most important consideration is that you are consistent.

ages of people and animals

Hyphenate ages when used before the noun:

a 7-year-old girl

In general, it is better to give ages in figures, otherwise you might end up with a combination of a hyphenated number with another hyphenated word, for example "a sixty-five-year-old man" when "a 65-year-old man" reads better.

Only hyphenate ages before the noun, not after:

the girl is seven years old

aging/ageing

Aging in American English, *ageing* in British English.

all right

Also spelled "alright." Be aware, however, that many dictionaries disapprove of the use of "alright." If in doubt, use "all right."

ALT text

Stands for "alternative text." It should be provided with every image on a Webpage, as it is particularly important for accessibility reasons. ALT text is contained in the HTML code and thus does not appear on the Webpage unless the cursor is held over the image and/or the image does not load properly.

Capitalize the first word only. No end punctuation (unless they are proper sentences):

Company office in New York

See also ACCESSIBILITY, GRAPHICS, LOGOS.

a.m./A.M./A.M.

Choose a style for your site and stick with it:

- lowercase with periods (*a.m.*—favored by the *Oxford English Dictionary*)
- capitals with periods (A.M.—favored by *The American Heritage Dictionary*)

- small capitals with periods (A.M.—favored by *The Chicago Manual of Style*)

American English

See LANGUAGE.

ampersand (&)

Don't use "&" unless it's part of a trademarked company name, for example Ernst & Young. An exception to this could be the use of the ampersand in navigation where there is no space for *and*.

analog

Not digital—data stored in a stream of continuous physical variables.

animation

Animation is useful if it significantly adds to the understanding of some concept or product. However, animation can negatively influence the readability of text nearby, because movement affects the eye's ability to focus. Therefore, an animation should either run a couple of times and stop, or have a command that allows readers to turn it off and on. In addition, animated content is generally much slower to download than ordinary text-based pages, and many readers associate animation with banner ads, which they tend to ignore. See also GRAPHICS, BANNER AD.

ANSI

ANSI (American National Standards Institute) is a private, non-profit organization responsible for approving US standards in many areas, including computers and communications. ANSI is the American representative of ISO. See also ISO.

apostrophe

Avoid apostrophes in plurals:

the 1990s *not* the 1990's
PCs *not* PC's
LANs, WANs, CPUs

Use apostrophes as grammatically required and remember the correct use of apostrophes in

women's, ladies', men's, children's, people's, each other's, one another's

See also POSSESSIVES.

applet

This is a small program that can be run in a browser or special applet viewer. For accessibility reasons, try to ensure that pages can still be viewed even if the reader's browser doesn't support applets.

See ACCESSIBILITY, JAVA.

archive

Traditionally refers to data that has been backed up, but increasingly in Internet terms it can also refer to non-recent content available on a site—the content that is stored in the body of the classification but not directly highlighted on the homepage. Don't remove old content that might still be of use to readers. Remove only content that is obviously out of date, such as an advertisement for a conference that has already been held.

See also CONTENT REVIEW.

articles (the, a, an)

An article signifies a noun. *The* is known as "the definite article," while *a* and *an* are the "indefinite articles."

Use *an* before words that begin with a vowel sound and words that begin with a silent *h*:

an enemy
an heir

Use *a* before a consonant sound, including an aspirated (pronounced) *h*:

a hero (not silent)
a union

Use *a* or *an* appropriately before abbreviations and acronyms. Remember, it depends on how it is pronounced:

a UN resolution (although UN starts with a vowel, it is not pronounced with a vowel sound—*you en*)

ASCII

Stands for American Standard Code for Information Interchange. ASCII is a code for representing English characters as numbers. ASCII files cannot contain any formatting commands (such as bold, italic, and so on); however, most computers can open an ASCII file. Plain-text files are in ASCII format.

ASP

1. Application Service Provider: a third-party company that hosts software applications and services for customer companies over a network.
2. Active Server Page: an HTML page that includes one or more small, embedded programs that are processed on a Microsoft Web server before the page is sent to the user.

assistive technology

This is software or hardware that has been specifically designed to assist people with disabilities to carry out daily activities. Assistive technology includes wheelchairs and reading machines. For the Web, common software-based assistive technologies include screen readers, screen magnifiers, speech synthesizers, and voice input software that operate in conjunction with graphical desktop browsers (among other user agents). Hardware assistive technologies include alternative keyboards and pointing devices. See also ACCESSIBILITY.

asynchronous

Not occurring at the same time, for example email, as opposed to synchronous communication, such as a chat room, which occurs in real time.

attachment

This is a file that is attached to an email, rather than being in the body of the email itself. The recipient must open the attachment to read its contents. The concern with attachments is the possible spread of viruses. Contrary to popular opinion, you cannot get a virus by simply receiving an email—it is only by opening an attachment that this is possible. To avoid email viruses, never open an attachment from somebody you don't know. Even then, be careful. Some viruses take over a person's email program and send themselves using that person's address (such as the LOVE BUG). Basically, if you're not expecting an attachment from someone, mail the sender to verify that the email is from that person.

Attachments can significantly add to the size of the email and therefore will take longer to download and open. In addition, the recipient must have the necessary software to open it. So don't send attachments unless you have to.

See also VIRUS.

attribution

If any material is repeated word for word from a published source, it should be identified as such. If the source document is on the Web, the simplest way to identify it is to include the URL. If the material is general in nature, it is permissible to rephrase it in your own words. What must be avoided is copying someone else's writing word for word.

Suppose a writer is mentioning the North American Free Trade Agreement (NAFTA) in an article, and has copied the following passage from brittanica.com into their notes:

> NAFTA's main provisions called for the gradual reduction of tariffs, customs duties, and other trade barriers between the three members, with some tariffs being removed immediately and others over periods of as long as 15 years.

There's nothing wrong with writing something like, "NAFTA was designed to gradually reduce trade barriers over a 15-year period," and no need to attribute it. There's also nothing wrong with repeating the entire description if it's preceded by a statement such as, "As described by brittanica.com ..." Offline sources must be described fully enough so that a reader can find them, and might include the names of the author, title of the work, the publisher, and date. Online sources should be directly linked to, preferably at the bottom of the document. See REFERENCING ONLINE SOURCES, PLAGIARISM.

Australian dollar

See FOREIGN CURRENCIES.

authentication

This is the process by which a person's credit card is checked.

authoring tool

Authoring tools include HTML editors, document conversion tools, and tools that generate Web content from databases.

autumn

Fall in American English, *autumn* in British English—lowercase in both.

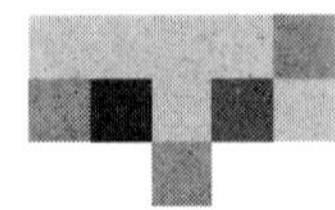

B2B

Business-to-business ecommerce—this is where businesses sell to other businesses over the Internet rather than through traditional channels.

B2C

Business-to-consumer ecommerce—this is the online retail of consumer goods and services. The most solid B2C model emerging is the clicks and mortar one. See CLICKS AND MORTAR.

B2G

Business-to-government ecommerce—this is where businesses sell to government or state agencies over the Internet.

backbone

See INTERNET BACKBONE.

Back button

A browser facility that allows the reader to "go back" to the last page they visited. The Back button is one of the most frequently used browser functions. "Hitting the Back button" has become a euphemism for getting out of a website.

The frequent use of the Back button shows the online reader's impatience. When designing a website, remember that the reader is a Back-button-click away from leaving. See ONLINE READER.

back end

Back end (noun), back-end (adjective).

Back-end software is software that runs on the mainframe or network server. Basically, the back end is the stuff that the reader doesn't see. The individual computer interacts with the front end, which in turn interacts with the back end. See also FRONT END.

background

Avoid tiled or otherwise distracting backgrounds (such as pictures used as backgrounds) because they make the text harder to read. See COLOR.

back up

Back up (verb), backup (noun and adjective).

This is when you make a duplicate copy of a program, a disk, or data. Always remember to back up, back up, and back up again.

backward, backwards

Backward in American English, *backwards* in British English.

backward compatible

This type of design continues to work with earlier versions of a language, program, or device.

bandwidth

Refers to the capacity of an electronic connection to send data. It is expressed in bits per second, bytes per second, or in hertz (cycles per second). The problem with bandwidth is that there's never enough of it. Most readers use modems to access the Internet and thus have low bandwidth connections, making things happen slower than they would like. Keep your pages as small as possible to avoid making your reader wait. See also BROADBAND, PAGE DOWNLOADS.

banner ad

A graphic advertisement on a website that Internet readers can click to go to the advertiser's site. Banners are often animated or interactive. Because an animated banner distracts a reader, a good policy is to have the banner animate only once. Banners can come in a number of sizes. However, the most common, generally found at the top of the page, is 468 × 60 pixels. Banners can slow down the loading of a page. Therefore most sites require that a banner is no larger than 8 KB in file size.

To have a faster download and thus better first impression for the reader, many websites avoid having banner ads on the homepage. Another option is to have a smaller banner ad on homepages.

See also PROMOTING CONTENT.

barter

A process where you swap content with other websites that are not directly competing with you.

basic search

See SEARCH.

beta

This is a pre-commercial release version of a piece of software. Companies allow people to download beta software for free or at a discount to get feedback on how well the software works.

best viewed with

An instruction found on some websites informing the reader that the website has been optimized for a particular browser or version of a browser. Also relates to informing the reader that they require some plug-in, such as Flash, to "best view" the website.

A best-viewed-with approach runs contrary to why the Web was invented in the first place. As Tim Berners-Lee, inventor of the Web, said in 1996: "Anyone who slaps a 'this page is best viewed with Browser X' label on a webpage appears to be yearning for the bad old days, before the Web, when you had very little chance of reading a document written on another computer, another word processor, or another network."

Put another way, this approach is a bit like telling a customer that your shop is best viewed with 3D glasses, and not just that, but you won't let them in unless they go off and buy a pair. It is rare indeed that you will find this elitist, reader-hostile approach to design in the more successful websites. A best-viewed-with approach to Web design is best viewed with skepticism.

billion

1,000 million. (Formerly in the UK, a billion represented one million million.)

The word *billion* is normally spelled out:

10 billion (not 10,000,000,000).

biographies

See BYLINES.

bit

Binary digit.

bitmap

A bitmap is a set of bits that represents a graphic image. Bitmaps are large files and are not generally used as a graphic format on the Web. See also JPEG, GIF.

bold

Be careful with any use of bold in the *body* of the text—large blocks of bold can be distracting, while a word in bold might be mistaken for a link. If you do use bold, ensure that it's black bold, as colored bold can easily be mistaken for a link. It's okay to use colored bold for a heading or subhead. See also COLOR.

bookmark

A bookmark is a shortcut to a Webpage, stored and accessed in a Web browser. In Microsoft Internet Explorer a bookmark is called a FAVORITE.

Boolean search

See SEARCH.

brackets

For punctuation information, see PARENTHESES AND PUNCTUATION.

branding

In the offline world, brands are increasingly driven by strong visual presentations that "grab" the reader's attention. On the Web, the reader must first find your website. Therefore, once at your site, your brand has already got your reader's attention, so don't annoy them by having a big swirling logo or a fancy splash screen that just delays them.

On a website, visual branding takes a backseat to content branding. Go to the websites of some of the biggest brands in the world (Microsoft, AOL, IBM) and you'll see small logos. Instead, they brand with their content, creating loyalty by providing easy-to-find, quality content. See also LOGOS, VIRAL MARKETING.

breadcrumb trail

See CLASSIFICATION PATH NAVIGATION.

breaking news

Breaking news deals with essential content that needs to be promoted immediately and as widely as possible throughout the website. To achieve this, a space directly underneath the masthead should be allocated. Breaking news should be text based.

Because breaking news is time-critical, not only the date but also hour and minute information should be provided. Always include the time zone. See also DATING DOCUMENTS AND SUMMARIES, PROMOTING CONTENT, TIME ZONES, MASTHEAD.

bricks and clicks

See CLICKS AND MORTAR.

bricks and mortar

This is a term for a traditional retail business.

British English

See LANGUAGE.

British pound

See FOREIGN CURRENCIES.

broadband

A high-speed communications technology that allows voice, Internet, and television to be delivered over one connection/wire. There is a danger that broadband has been massively over-hyped. In 1996, we were told that broadband was "just around the corner." In 2000, we were told that broadband was "just around the corner." Studies are indicating that even by 2005 the average person accessing the Internet will not have broadband access. So don't design your site on the assumption that everybody will soon have broadband access—they may be waiting a while yet.

brochureware

A website that is basically an imitation of a brochure, employing little or none of the unique characteristics of the Web (hypertext, comprehensive updated content, interactivity, search).

browser

See WEB BROWSER.

browser compatibility

Refers to whether a website is viewable in a range of browsers. Different browsers—in fact different versions of different browsers—can present Webpages in very different ways. A webpage that looks fine on Internet Explorer 5, for example, may look terrible in Netscape Navigator 4. It's vital that a website design works well in all major browsers and browser versions. The only way to determine this is to test the website on a variety of browser versions. As a rule of thumb, your website should work with all browsers of version 4 and upward.

browser window

See WINDOW.

browsing

The act of using a browser to move from website to website, or to move through a particular website.

bulletin board

See DISCUSSION BOARD.

buttons

Capitalize the first word only.

Submit your comments

When referring to button names in the body text, follow the interface for capitalization style, that is, if it's capitalized on the interface, then capitalize it in the text:

> Click the Print button on the Standard toolbar to print your file.

See also ONSCREEN CAPITALIZATION.

bylines

Readers like to know who the author of a particular article is. They may also wish to find out more about that author, and perhaps get in touch with them. Therefore, it is advisable to provide a byline for each document (By John Smith). Have the byline link to an email address. Also provide a "Bio" link beside the byline that links to biographical details, such as other articles they have written. Provide a photo of the author where possible.

The recommended position is after the heading and summary and before the body of the article, in the same size as the body text.

byte

A group of eight bits.

C

C2C

Consumer-to-consumer ecommerce—this is where consumers sell directly to other consumers over the Internet, usually on an auction site such as eBay.

cable modem

A modem offering high-speed Internet access over cable television lines.

cache

Webpages you request are stored in your browser's cache directory on your hard disk. A cache speeds up download times because the browser can get files from the cache directory rather than the Web server.

calendar of events

A tool used to maintain an efficient commissioning process for content. A calendar of events lists key upcoming events or subject areas that the organization must create content for, and may look forward one week, one month, or one year, depending on the nature of the organization.

Time and time again the problem a website faces is neither design nor technology related, it's not having the content completed on time. If you don't plan for new content and actively follow up with writers, it won't get delivered when you want it. A calendar of events should contain the reason for commissioning the content; a description of what is required and the number of words required; the due date; the resource requirements; and the writer(s) responsible.

Canadian dollar

See FOREIGN CURRENCIES.

cannibalization

This refers to what occurs when companies lose customers from their traditional outlets to their Web outlets so that there is no net gain in customers.

capitalization

Specific capitalization style is given throughout this guide. In general, avoid over-capitalization. The current practice is toward using lowercase unless there's a compelling reason for capitalizing. This style is also less distracting on a Webpage and allows readers to scan more easily.

Write sentences to avoid the use of a case-sensitive lowercase word (for example, a product name or command) at the beginning.

cascading style sheets

See CSS.

catalog, catalogue

Catalog in American English, *catalogue* in British English.

categorization

See CLASSIFICATION.

CD-ROM

Compact disc read-only memory.

cell phone

Short for cellular phone, referred to as *mobile phones* or *mobiles* in Europe.

centuries

In general, spell out references to particular centuries in lowercase (numerals may be used in headings):

> the seventeenth century

Hyphenate the adjectival form:

> twentieth-century architecture

CGI

Acronym for Common Gateway Interface, a means for a Web server to transfer a reader's request to an application program and to receive data back to return to the reader.

characteristics of online readers

See ONLINE READER.

chat

A real-time text-based conversation between people on the Internet.

chat rooms

The virtual "rooms" that readers chat in. Typically these "real-time" discussion areas involve a relatively small number (2 to 20) of simultaneous readers per chat room. By their very nature, they tend to be far more ad hoc, spontaneous, and informal than DISCUSSION BOARDS.

This real-time form of communication means online chat tends to be more appropriate for socially oriented websites such as entertainment sites. It is also suitable for one-off events, or sites behind a subscription/registration barrier that allow the population to be better defined and controlled, such as online focus groups, brainstorming-type meetings within your own organization, and so on.

checkboxes

Capitalize the first word and proper nouns only. Don't use end punctuation unless it's a complete sentence.

☐ **Exact word matches only**
☐ **Include word variants**

Chinese yuan

See FOREIGN CURRENCIES.

circular linking

See LINKS, LOGOS.

citations

See REFERENCING ONLINE SOURCES.

classification

Also referred to as "taxonomy" and "categorization," classification is about organizing content in a logical manner so the reader can find what they are looking for quickly and efficiently. The classic example of classification is the Dewey Decimal Classification system, used by libraries worldwide. Without it, libraries would be chaotic places (just like much of the Web, really).

The more content you have, and the more readers you have, the more you require a classification system. Yahoo is a perfect example of the commercial benefits of having a well-structured directory classification. (Classification and navigation are very much intertwined. See NAVIGATION.)

The Internet has been described as a giant library with all the books on the floor and the lights turned out. Proper classification turns on the lights and puts the "books" in their proper place. A well-thought-out classification system is essential to the success of any website. It allows the organization to efficiently organize content, helps the reader to find content quickly and easily, and puts the content into context.

- **General standards:** Classify for the reader, not for some internal and perhaps idiosyncratic organizational structure. All classification names should be short and exact. Don't classify deeper than five levels, as most people will not click further than that to find content. Ideally, three levels should be sufficient. Avoid having more than 40 documents per classification (or else subdivide).
- **Clutter is preferable to clicking:** The breadth of the classification system should be easy to display. Ideally, all top levels should be viewable at the same time, without scrolling. A general guideline of no more than 15 top-level classifications should apply (10 or less would be ideal). However, on the Web, people prefer clutter to clicking. In other words, they prefer to see a page with lots of links, once it's well organized, than an elegant page that forces them to click to another level to find the link they are looking for. Remember, always avoid wasting the reader's time.

classification path navigation

This navigation (also called a history trail, cookie trail, or breadcrumb trail) tells you exactly what part of the site you are in and how that relates to the overall classification system.

Classification path navigation is probably not necessary for small websites. As a rule, the more content on a website, the more important it is to have such navigation. Where core navigation is being employed, classification path navigation becomes essential. See CORE NAVIGATION.

Classification path navigation should be placed just below the masthead, aligned tight to the left of the page. It should begin with the homepage and show all levels down to where the document has been found. Thus, it should always begin with "Home."

Each classification should link back to that particular section in the classification. The final classification should not be linked, as this is where the reader is, and linking it would just bring it back to itself. However, it should be made bold to give more indication of where the reader is. It may also be a different color.

Home > Products > **Product XY**

Yahoo places the final classification (in this example, "Ancient History") on a separate line to help the reader clearly identify the section they are in:

Home > Arts > Humanities > History > By Time Period >
Ancient History

See also NAVIGATION.

click

A single instance of pressing and releasing the button on a mouse or other pointing device on a computer. On a Webpage, clicking a link will move the reader to wherever the link directs them, while clicking a button on their browser can move them off your site altogether.

click here

The use of phrases such as "click here" or "click for more" are generally frowned on and are unnecessary if you make the hyperlinked text self-explanatory, as you should endeavor to do.

A "click here" approach can be applied within a banner ad, or where you want the reader to carry out a specific action. For example, "To download our free software, please click here." You could also use it where the target reader is a relative novice and may not be familiar with hypertext. See also LINKS, LINK TITLES.

click-through

Every time a reader clicks an online advertisement and is brought to the advertiser's website, it is counted as a click-through. This method of charging for advertising is controversial, as it does not measure the number of people who have been exposed to the ad.

clicks and mortar

Refers to any retail company that has taken advantage of the Internet to create an online presence in addition to its existing offline retail presence. This strategy is seen as more cost effective, marketing efficient, and consumer friendly than a pure-play strategy. The bookseller Barnes and Noble is an example of a clicks and mortar company. Interchangeable with bricks and clicks. See also PURE-PLAY.

client

On the Internet, a client is a computer that accesses shared network resources provided by another computer called the server. See SERVER.

client side

Occurring on the client side of a client/server system. Client-side image maps, for example, are executed by the code within the Webpage itself, whereas a server-side image map requires reference to a separate file on the Web server every time a user clicks an image map. CGI scripts are server-side applications (they run on the Web server), while JavaScript scripts are client-side (they are executed by your browser).

Client-side image maps are preferable for faster downloads and accessibility reasons. See also ACCESSIBILITY, IMAGE MAP, SERVER SIDE.

collaborative content

Collaborative content is content that is created by more than one person. Collaboratively created content is a major trend of the future, driven by digital format and, in particular, the Internet with its speed, cost efficiency, common medium and tools, and easily modified and reproducible content.

Collaborative writing works well when there is a major content-creation task at hand that ideally demands the input of multiple disciplines and is separable into clearly defined segments that can be allocated to individual writers. Organizations that have a well-thought-out set of processes to facilitate collaboration can benefit from it most.

However, merely allocating people pieces of work is not collaboration. Unless there is strong interaction between writers, and an overall sense of direction and style is jointly established, you will not achieve the true potential of collaboration. For it to work, management must be behind it, and a genuine respect, understanding, and shared enthusiasm must exist between the writers.

collective nouns

Collective nouns refer to groups of animate beings, such as committee, company, government, the aristocracy. They are singular nouns even though they have a plural connotation, and consequently take singular verbs and pronouns (*is*, *it*):

> The company *is* based in the US. *It* has offices in New York.
>
> His audience *was* not sympathetic.

Collective nouns are used when the group is considered as a unified body. When, occasionally, the noun is clearly and unmistakably used to refer to the separate individuals within the group, plural verbs and pronouns can be used:

> The audience *were* asked to remain in *their* seats.

Make sure agreement is consistent. Do not mix singulars and plurals:

> **Incorrect:** The union *is* determined to protect *their* rights [should be *its* rights].

See MAJORITY, PERCENT, PERCENTAGE, COMPANIES.

colons (:)

The colon is introductory and is used within a sentence to signal that what comes after it explains, interprets, or amplifies what has preceded it. Do not confuse the colon with the semicolon, which generally separates parallel parts of a sentence.

> There was only one thing left to do: run.

The colon is also used to introduce long direct quotations (use a comma when the quotation is short and remains within the paragraph).

Use a colon to introduce a list only when it is required by grammar, that is, when the text following the colon does not flow naturally from it. The flow is normally broken by a phrase such as "the following." For the use of a colon in displayed lists, see LISTS.

> Please bring the following: pen, pencil, paper, clipboard, and eraser. (Colon necessary)

> Please bring a pen, pencil, paper, clipboard, and eraser. (Colon unnecessary)

Lastly, the colon is used to separate elements such as numerals in clock time (particularly in the US, *3:30* A.M.) and in ratios.

In general, don't capitalize the word following a colon unless the word is a proper noun, or unless what follows the colon is a complete sentence.

See also SEMICOLONS, QUOTATIONS.

color, colour

Color in American English, *colour* in British English.

Early Webpages tended to be awash with color—colored type, colored backgrounds, and colored type on colored backgrounds, textures, and shadings. If anything, it became unusual to find white space on websites. The problem with this was, and is, that colored type is often more difficult to read than black type, especially on a colored background.

Black type on a white background (85 percent white is optimal) has emerged as a de facto standard on most professionally published websites. Though you still see lots of unreadable color schemes on Webpages, especially on self-consciously hip and artsy sites, amateur sites, and (inexplicably) corporate sites, you won't find them on any of the Web's most-trafficked and therefore most successful websites. The best-practice standard is that white or light backgrounds rule, and that black or dark type is right. See also BACKGROUND, WHITE SPACE.

column

An area of defined space going vertically down a Webpage. The general convention is that Webpages should have three columns, although for presentation purposes a document page may have two. See HOMEPAGE DESIGN, WEBSITE LAYOUT AND DESIGN.

comma

Many people find using the comma one of the most confusing areas of punctuation. While we cannot outline the full range of comma use here (please consult any good style or usage guide, such as *The Chicago Manual of Style* or *The American Heritage Book of English Usage*), we have included some guidance on those points that frequently cause writers to slip up.

- **Lists:** A comma is used to break up lists in a series of three or more items. The main question here is whether to use a comma before the last item in a list. In general, a comma is used before the final *and/or* in a list in American English, and generally avoided in British English (unless it would lead to confusion).

  Red, white, and blue (American English)
  Red, white and blue (British English)

- **Dates:** When you are displaying the day, month, and year in American English, set off the year with commas:

  August 10, 2001, was the day in question.

- **Direct quotations:** Use a comma before a direct quotation of only a few words following an introductory phrase (use a colon before long direct quotations):

  She said, "Now or never."

- **Appositives:** Use a comma with appositives (a noun or noun phrase that means the same as the noun beside it):

  My mother, Sue, owns a shop. (I have only one mother. If the name "Sue" was omitted, it would still be clear to whom I was referring.)

The CEO, John Brown, called the meeting. (Similarly, there's only one CEO.)

But restrictive or defining appositives are not set off by commas:

My friend Sue owns a shop. (In this instance, as I have many friends, if "Sue" were not included, it would not be clear to whom I referred.)

- **Parenthetic expressions:** Use a pair of commas to enclose a parenthetic expression (an expression that says something non-essential about the subject—if you take away the commas and the statement inside them, the sentence should still make sense). One of the most frequent errors in punctuation is to forget one of these commas.

  Correct: My mother, who will be 55 this year, jogs every day.
  Incorrect: My mother, who will be 55 this year jogs every day.

- **Introductory words or phrases:** A comma is often used after introductory words or phrases (Alternatively, However, Generally, Indeed):

  Alternatively, you can apply in writing.

- **Adverbial clauses and phrases:** Use a comma after adverbial clauses and phrases (unless they can be clearly read without a comma):

  Having ascended the mountain, we stopped to admire the view.

  However, do not use a comma after an adverbial phrase if the phrase immediately precedes the main verb:

  Beside the house was a garage.

- **Between certain clauses:** Use a comma after certain introductory dependent clauses (if, when, for, etc.) and between two independent clauses connected by a coordinate conjunction (but, for, so, and, nor, etc.):

If you leave now, you will lose your money.
He knew little, and he said less.

However, when the independent clauses are closely related, you do not need a comma:

The sun was shining and my clothes were drying.

Commas are sometimes used to separate main clauses that are not joined by conjunctions (connecting words such as *and*, *but*, *as*, *because*)—especially with short or parallel sentences.

One day it rained, the next day it poured.

- **Between coordinate adjectives:** Use a comma between two or more adjectives when each adjective qualifies the noun equally, for example:

  a brilliant, talented writer

  But when the adjective closer to the noun has more importance, no comma is used, for example:

  a studious law student

  An easy way to establish whether adjectives are coordinating or not is to test whether you can change the order of the adjectives and whether you can replace the comma with *and* without changing the meaning. If it is not changed, they are coordinating and a comma should be used.

  a brilliant and talented writer
  a talented, brilliant writer
  (no change, therefore coordinate)
  a studious and law student
  a law, studious student
  (doesn't work, therefore not coordinate)

commissioning content

Content is commissioned when the editor recognizes a need for a certain type of content that will be created only if it is actively commissioned from internal staff or freelance writers. Which path is taken depends on the staff having both the required knowledge or skills and the time to create the required content. The disadvantages of using freelance writers are that it can be a time-consuming process for the editor to find the right people, and while it can be cost-effective for small quantities of content, it can get expensive where larger quantities are involved.

community

See ONLINE COMMUNITY.

companies

Companies are singular and take singular verbs and pronouns:

> Microsoft is (not *are*) launching a new Internet product.

They are entities, not people, so don't use 'who' to refer to a company:

> Amazon.com is a site that (not *who*) knows how to sell.

Company names are normally trademarked and the companies themselves will normally have guidelines on how they would like you to spell their name. It's normally the full legal name they want, for example *Microsoft Corporation*. It depends on how formal your approach is in deciding whether to list the full legal name rather than the more common name, *Microsoft*. Some financial websites will list the full legal name in the first reference, whereas a more general site might choose to list the common form of the name. Any legal documents or press releases should list the full legal name.

In general, you should refer to the company name as the company does itself in terms of capitalization and punctuation (for example, AltaVista has a capital *V* in the middle of its name). However, some companies use conventions that make it difficult to incorporate it into text. For example, many company names now start with a lowercase letter, such as eBay. We would advise rewriting the sentence so that the name doesn't appear at the beginning of the sentence, or if it must remain there, capitalize the letter, no matter what the company does—otherwise, it just looks wrong. Similarly, adding the exclamation mark to Yahoo's name can make your text look as if you're shouting at the reader. See COLLECTIVE NOUNS.

comprise

Comprise means to "contain" or "include all" and is best used in the active voice:

> Great Britain comprises England, Scotland, Wales, and Northern Ireland.

The use of comprise in the passive to mean "consist of" is largely frowned on, for example:

> **Incorrect:** Great Britain is comprised of England, Scotland, Wales, and Northern Ireland.

In general, avoid using "comprised of." Use "composed of" instead.

computer keys/onscreen commands

Computer keys referred to in text should take an initial cap, for example:

> Press Enter
> Select Open from the File menu

confirmation message

This is an email that someone who has just subscribed to a subscription service receives, usually after responding to a verification message. The confirmation message should contain general information on the subscription service. Specifically, it should contain the email address the reader subscribed with; the username and password if these are required; and clear unsubscription and subscription details. The reader should be advised to store this message for future reference. See DOUBLE OPT-IN, SUBSCRIPTION-BASED PUBLISHING, VERIFICATION MESSAGE.

consistency

Whether dealing with style and usage or the design of your site, ensure you are consistent. Creating your own style guide will help ensure consistency in your written content. Choose a dictionary that all contributors to your site will use as a main reference.

Consistency in layout, navigation, and design will greatly enhance your site, both visually and in terms of usability.

See also WEBSITE LAYOUT AND DESIGN, STYLE GUIDE, NAVIGATION.

contact information

Always offer contact details (including information about your physical location), ideally in the footer of every page. If you have more than one office, have a contact link. See also FORMS, FOOTER.

content

Content is knowledge that has been formally produced into a media such as text, graphics, video, animation, and so on. The reason the Internet was invented was to communicate content. The reason the Web was invented was to publish content.

content acquisition

Getting quality content and maintaining that standard should be the primary aim of your site (as well as having the information architecture in place to facilitate finding and reading that content). In an ideal world, you would identify lots of high-quality content to deliver to the reader. However, quality content is expensive and we must all accept the reality that there will be a trade-off between the ultimate set of content and the cost of generating such content. What is important is to identify the "must-have" as against the "like-to-have" content.

There are a number of steps involved in acquiring content.

- **Reader identification:** You need to identify your reader before deciding what content to present them with. See READER IDENTIFICATION.

- **Content identification:** Once you've identified the reader, you must identify the content you need to deliver to that reader. Remember, get the reader wrong and you're wasting your time. Get the content wrong for the reader and you're wasting both your time and theirs! See also FORMATS.
- **Creating original content:** Creating content written specifically for your readers and in a proper Web format is the ideal solution, but remember that quality original content is very expensive.
- **Reusing content:** The Holy Grail for many technologists is a situation where content is created once and then reused in a wide variety of media: the Web, email, print, and so on. This shows a fundamental lack of understanding of content and the way people read content. People read content differently on the Web, in newspapers, in magazines, in books, in reports.

  Reusing content written for one media in another, without at least some editing of that content, is delivering second-hand content to the reader. Although second-hand content has its place, if a reader is expecting quality content that is specifically written for the media they are using, they will be less than happy with finding content prepared for another media. Think of receiving a 5,000-word report on your cell phone.

  By all means take the content you have already produced, but reformat it appropriately for the Web and for email. This is significantly cheaper than creating content from scratch. See Section I, "Writing for the Web," to find out how to do this. Also, there is already a huge quantity of content on the Internet. Summarize it, quote it, editorialize on it, link to it, and compare one view to another. (But avoid plagiarism—see PLAGIARISM.)
- **Content conversion:** In most environments, there will be sizable quantities of content that the organization has already created. For cost and time reasons, it may not be practical for the organization to rewrite all this content specifically for the Web. Therefore, a technical approach may be required to convert, for example, Excel spreadsheets into a Web-based table layout.

When converting content, you should ask yourself who is actually going to read this content. Converting content without a target reader in mind only adds to information overload. In publishing, more is invariably less.

- **Purchasing content:** There may well be news feeds, reports, or other content available for purchase that can provide valuable content for your website. It is often cheaper to pay copyright fees for these than to write the content from scratch.
- **Reviewing content:** It is essential to review already published content regularly. See CONTENT REVIEW.

content conversion

See CONTENT ACQUISITION.

content creation

See CONTENT ACQUISITION.

content identification

See CONTENT ACQUISITION

content layout

See WEBSITE LAYOUT AND DESIGN.

content management

Content management refers to the processes involved in managing content on a website. In its broadest sense, content management is synonymous with publishing, in that it deals with the creation, editing, and publishing of content. In its narrowest sense, content management is associated with the pure processes involved in creating and storing content. In this narrow definition, content management does not concern itself with whether content is well written or well presented, merely that there are processes in place for moving, storing, and searching for content.

content purchase

See CONTENT ACQUISITION.

content review

The process by which content that is published is reviewed to see whether it should remain published. Review is critical on a website. Otherwise, content will remain on the website long after it has gone out of date. (Many articles should still be available online long after they were published, but content such as a holiday notice or a special deal should be removed once the relevant time has passed.) The review process can work in a number of ways:

- **Expiry date:** An expiration date can be set for the content when it is published, which removes it from publication once that date has been reached.
- **Updates:** As new content is prepared for publication, it is compared with similar content already published with a view to removing that content if it is now out of date.
- **Periodic reviews:** A periodic review process is established whereby after a defined period (6 months, 12 months), all content is reviewed to check its relevance.

contractions

Contractions are shortened forms of a word or words, such as *he's* for *he is*.

Do not feel as though you cannot use them on the Web—or, in other words, don't feel that you can't use them. They tend to add a somewhat conversational flavor to the writing, though like all grammatical devices, their use depends on the context.

No periods are needed after words that are shortened by using at least their first and last letters, for example

Mr, Ltd, Dept

See also TONE.

convergence

The coming together of two or more distinct technologies. Usually refers to the merging of television, Internet services, and cell phones. Convergence is seen as a Holy Grail of the new economy. Steve Case, chairman of AOL Time Warner, has said that if the 1980s was the decade of the PC, and the 1990s was the decade of the Internet, then the 2000s would be the decade of convergence. "The lines between those devices are blurring, and the distinctions between the industries servicing those devices are blurring as well," he told the J.P. Morgan H&Q Technology Conference in May 2001.

cookie

A piece of software that resides on a browser containing personal information on the user of the browser, such as passwords, personal details, what websites they have visited. This information is used by the organization that created the cookie to recognize readers the next time they visit the website and to track them, thus building up a profile of the reader.

The benefits of cookies for readers include not having to continuously re-enter their passwords, and having personalized webpages. Worries about privacy issues constitute the main drawback. Therefore, a reader's permission should be sought before placing a cookie on their browser. See also PRIVACY.

cookie trail

See CLASSIFICATION PATH NAVIGATION.

copyeditor

The final step in ensuring that the content is understandable and readable is copyediting (known as subediting in Britain). The person filling this role may rearrange sentences and paragraphs and rewrite them to eliminate awkwardness and imprecision. The copyeditor should also check spelling and grammar. The copyeditor ideally should act as the champion of the reader, looking at each piece of content afresh and eliminating impediments to readability. During copyediting, the metadata should be checked to ensure its accuracy. See METADATA.

copyright

A copyright notice such as "Copyright © 1995–2001 Example Company. All rights reserved" should appear in the footer information of every page and link to a separate page for legal information (including trademarks and copyrights) or to a section of the Terms of use statement if one exists.

The copyright page should clearly state the conditions under which the organization's content can be used by third parties, and the procedure which a third party must undertake to acquire copyright permission. This copyright page should include the legal name of the company, group name if part of a group, reader agreement if any, and information on any company trademarks.

See FOOTER, TERMS OF USE STATEMENT.

core navigation

Core navigation is where the main body of classification is represented. An example of core navigation is found at Yahoo—"Arts and Culture," "Business," and so on (see Figure 3.1). Once established, avoid changing core navigation, particularly the top level. Core navigation is for websites that have a substantial quantity of content. For smaller websites, it may be sufficient to use only a global navigation.

FIGURE 3.1

Arts & Humanities Literature, Photography...	**News & Media** Full Coverage, Newspapers, TV...
Business & Economy B2B, Finance, Shopping, Jobs...	**Recreation & Sports** Sports, Travel, Autos, Outdoors...
Computers & Internet Internet, WWW, Software, Games...	**Reference** Libraries, Dictionaries, Quotations...
Education College and University, K-12...	**Regional** Countries, Regions, US States...
Entertainment Cool Links, Movies, Humor, Music...	**Science** Animals, Astronomy, Engineering...
Government Elections, Military, Law, Taxes...	**Social Science** Archaeology, Economics, Languages...
Health Medicine, Diseases, Drugs, Fitness...	**Society & Culture** People, Environment, Religion...

An example of core navigation from the Yahoo website.

Depending on the quantity of content to be classified, the core navigation may be broken up. For example, Dell presents two types of core navigation on its homepage: product-focused and customer-segment focused.

The core navigation tends to be placed in the left column of the page. In directory-type websites, where there is a substantial number of classifications, you may find the core navigation placed in the center column. Wherever it is placed, always try to ensure that as much of the core navigation as possible is seen from the first screen.

The core navigation should ideally be presented as hypertext. Always try to get each classification on one line (by shortening words if necessary). However, if a classification name is going to wrap over two lines, put bullet points or other markers in front of all the classification names. This ensures that the reader will not be confused into thinking that a classification that has stretched to two lines is in fact two separate classifications.

See also GLOBAL NAVIGATION, NAVIGATION.

corporations

See COMPANIES.

corrections

It is necessary to have a correction process in place to deal with any situation where incorrect and/or illegal content is published on the website. Deal with corrections as a matter of urgency, as they are likely to mislead the reader, and in certain circumstances may lead to libel or safety issues.

Your correction policy should state how you will deal with errors, ranging from the minor grammatical-type mistakes to the very serious factual errors that may lead to a libel case or constitute a danger of some kind.

With minor errors, it is not necessary to publicly note that you have changed the document, but for more serious errors, you should at the very least note the correction and state why it was made and, if required, remove the document and/or publish an apology. See also LIBEL.

counter

See PAGE COUNTER.

CPM

Stands for cost per mille (thousand), the method of pricing advertising by charging per thousand impressions (views). See IMPRESSION.

cracker

A criminal or malicious hacker. See HACKER.

crash

A crash occurs when the computer system has a serious failure. The system either stops working totally (hangs), or a particular program crashes (stops working).

CRM

Stands for customer relationship management, a term for the software and other technologies that allow organizations to manage customer relationships in an organized way before, during, and after a sale occurs.

CSS

Short for cascading style sheet, a feature added to HTML that allows authors of HTML documents and readers to attach style sheets to HTML documents, and thus have more control over how pages are displayed. They can also be built into user agents. The style sheets include typographical information on how the page should appear, such as the text font, headers, and links. These style sheets can then be applied to any Webpage. See also ACCESSIBILITY.

currencies

See FOREIGN CURRENCIES.

customization

Refers to changing a generic product in order to suit a customer's particular needs.

cyber

A prefix meaning "online" or "digital."

cybercrime

One word.

cyberspace

This refers to *all* computer networks, but specifically the Internet. Originally coined by William Gibson in his 1984 book *Neuromancer* (Ace Books, 2000): "Cyberspace: a consensual hallucination experienced daily by billions of legitimate operators ... A graphic representation of data abstracted from the banks of every computer in the human system." The Internet has yet to live up to Gibson's descriptions.

cybersquatting

Occurs when someone registers a domain name with the aim of profiting by selling the address to its rightful owner. See also TYPOSQUATTING, WIPO.

D

dash

Generally, dashes are used in text to indicate a break in thought or sentence structure, to separate two clauses, or to introduce a phrase added for emphasis, definition, or explanation. They can be used singly or in pairs. British English commonly uses an en dash (–), while the longer em dash

(—) is the standard dash in American English. As dashes can get lost on screen, the best dash to use is the longest, the em dash, in general onscreen text. It should have no spaces between it and the letters beside it.

> The dog—having been bred in the country—was uneasy in the city.
> I was amazed to see her there—she never goes out.

Do not capitalize the word following an em dash unless it is a proper noun, even if the text following the em dash is a complete sentence.

Use an unspaced double hyphen (--) for plain-text formats, such as email newsletters.

Use an en dash (–) in spans of figures, in expressions relating to time or distance, and to express an association between words that retain their separate identity in a compound adjective:

> 1945–9
> the Anglo–Irish Agreement
> pages 306–7

Never use an en dash with the words "from" and "between":

> **Incorrect:** between 1970–90

data

Data, in computer terms, is treated as a collective noun and is therefore used with singular verbs and pronouns (see COLLECTIVE NOUNS):

> This data is inconclusive.

Data is a type of content that is generally produced as a result of a defined and repeatable computer-based process. Data is factual and tends to be number-based rather than text-based. For example, the output from software that tracks website visitors can be described as "website log data."

Data is either right or wrong. For example, "Website Visitors: 1,897" is either right or wrong. You can interpret data and create "richer" content, but data itself is not an interpretation. Generally, data in its raw state tends to be voluminous and contains irrelevant as well as relevant content. Therefore, it needs to be interpreted and edited to create content that is useful to the more general reader. See also CONTENT, INFORMATION, KNOWLEDGE.

database

A software system that stores content and allows for its retrieval through a classification scheme and/or search engine. A database facilitates the creation of processes that allow content to be created, stored, modified, deleted, searched, and published.

data management

Data management fundamentally focuses on storing content. It is not concerned with whether the content is useful. A historical problem with data management revolved around the fact that merely storing content didn't always mean it could be efficiently retrieved at some future date.

The deficiencies with data management have led to the emergence of content management and publishing approaches to content. See CONTENT MANAGEMENT, PUBLISHING.

data mining

The process by which large quantities of generally statistical-type data is analyzed to discover trends that will allow the organization to make its processes more efficient and targeted. A typical data mining trend would be: "Women tend to buy from the website at weekends."

dates

Lay out dates as follows:

- **American English:** Although not universal, the standard form is generally month-day-year. In this style, you must set off the year with commas.

  Thursday, May 3, 2001, was a great day.

  The comma following the year can be omitted if it is replaced by some other form of punctuation, such as a period, semicolon, or dash:

  I will always remember Thursday, May 3, 2001.

If you have just the month and year, do not separate them with a comma:

November 2000

- **British English:** Standard British style is day-month-year, with no internal punctuation:

  3 May 2001

Use names of months rather than numbers, as 11-3-2001 means November 3 in American English and March 11 in British English. Instead, abbreviate the name of the month if necessary (see MONTHS):

Jan. 10, 2001

Another option is to use the recommendation of the International Organization for Standardization (ISO), which presents dates in the form year-month-date, separated by hyphens:

2001-05-29

Pairs of dates are shortened using an en dash to the shortest pronounceable form:

1991–5, *but* 1915–18, 1998–2002

Where a single year, such as a financial year, is spread over two or more calendar years, use a forward slash (also known as a solidus or an oblique stroke):

1992/3

Years are expressed in figures, but avoid starting a sentence with a figure (see NUMBERS). Rephrase instead. So,

2001 was a bad year for tech stocks

becomes

The year 2001 was a bad year for tech stocks

Abbreviate years as follows:

He was born in '92

Use *s* without an apostrophe to indicate decades or centuries:

1990s
1900s

See also NUMBERS, CENTURIES, DECADES.

dating documents and summaries

Most, but not all, documents and stand-alone summaries on a website will need to be dated. Some will even need hour and minute information.

You need to consider whether the date is relevant to the document and whether dating the document will help the reader. Hour and minute information will also be necessary if the document is a time-critical one, such as breaking news. (If using hour and minute information, make sure you include the time zone, as the Internet is a global medium.)

Some documents will not require a date and might be considered "timeless" in a sense. For example, an FAQ page or a document such as "Ten things to know about email" would not need to be dated as it will stay on the site as long as it is relevant. Dating it might make it look "old" in the sense of "out of date" when in fact it simply does not require updating, and more importantly, adding the date does not benefit the reader in any way. Another example of a "timeless" piece might be a company info page that simply gives a run-down on when the company was founded and what its aims are.

In a homepage or similar environment where the summary stands alone, place the date at the beginning of the summary (see Figure 3.2). You can use the abbreviated form of the month (Nov. 6, 2000,) for space reasons here if required. (See MONTHS for the proper abbreviations.)

In the document itself, present the date in its unabbreviated form (November 6, 2000,) above the document heading, preferably in the same size font as the body text. In long documents, the date should also appear under the author's name at the very end of the document. See WEBSITE LAYOUT AND DESIGN for an example. See also DATES, MONTHS, TIME ZONES.

FIGURE 3.2

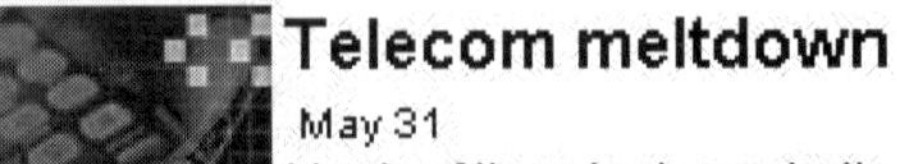

Telecom meltdown

May 31

Much of the stock market's recent bad news centers on the telecommunications industry, which has weakened tremendously, especially the new companies it spawned in recent years. (full story)

An example of a stand-alone summary on CNN

decades

Decades may be spelled out, in lowercase:

the seventies

Alternatively, they can be given in numerals with apostrophes:

the '70s

If the decade is identified by its century, it's usual practice to use numerals (without apostrophes):

the 1970s

deep linking

Deep linking occurs when a reader clicks a link on one website and is brought to a page "deep" into another website rather than to the homepage of the second website. The potential problem with deep linking is its overuse. If you make a large number of links deep into another website, legally it could be seen that you are attempting to pass off that website's content as your own. Thus, the use of a large number of links deep into another website should be avoided.

default homepage

This is the page that is automatically shown when the browser loads. Studies have found that a large number of readers don't know they can change this page. It's important, particularly within an intranet environment, to ensure that the technical department responsible for installing browsers makes sure that the default homepage is that of the relevant homepage.

deleting content

See CONTENT REVIEW.

denial-of-service attack

Usually intentional or malicious, a denial-of-service attack occurs when an organization experiences a temporary loss of all network connectivity or loses some of its services such as email. The most common form of attack occurs when a network is purposely flooded with extra information requests to the point where it cannot handle those requests and crashes. Although this kind of security breach doesn't normally involve the theft of or risk to information, it can still cost a lot in time, money, and potential lost customers.

design

See Section II, "Designing for the Web."

See also CLASSIFICATION, NAVIGATION, WEBSITE LAYOUT AND DESIGN.

desktop

One word as both noun and adjective. This can refer to an onscreen work area that uses icons and menus to simulate the top of a desk, such as those used in the Apple Macintosh and Microsoft Windows operating systems. It can also refer to a desktop computer—a personal computer that fits neatly on a desk.

Deutsche Mark

See FOREIGN CURRENCIES.

DHTML

Dynamic HTML allows a Webpage to change each time it is viewed. There are many technologies for producing dynamic HTML, including CGI scripts, cascading style sheets, and cookies. It also refers to new HTML extensions that will enable a Webpage to react to reader input without sending requests to the Web server.

dialup, dial up

One word as an adjective, two words as verb:

> Most people use dialup access to view Webpages.
> You can dial up the Internet using your phone line.

(The reason it has to remain two words as a verb is that otherwise you cannot create the past tense, *dialed up*.)

dialup access

Refers to connecting an access device to a network over telephone lines for a limited time.

different from/than

Traditional guidelines advise using *different from* when the comparison is between two persons or things, and *different than* when the object of the comparison is expressed in a full clause. However, never use *different than* in British English. Do not use *different to* at all.

> My boots are different *from* his.
>
> Working in the hotel was different *than* it was in Australia.

See also PREPOSITIONS TO WATCH.

digital age

An age in civilization where the key means of production are digital. See also NEW ECONOMY.

digital divide

The social and economic gap between those who have access to the Internet and other communications technologies, and those who do not. The indications are that the Internet and computers have in fact widened the disparity between rich and poor. Not only do poorer countries have far fewer resources to make proper use of technology, but even in wealthy countries, disadvantaged schools often continue to lose out, further disadvantaging their students.

directory

A directory is a way of organizing content generally using some sort of A to Z structure. On the Web, directories have become associated with a human-based approach to classification, rather than a purely technological approach.

For example, Yahoo is a search directory that is designed and managed by editors and classification experts. AltaVista, on the other hand, started off as a search "engine," depending on software to index the Web. See Section II, "Designing for the Web" for more information. See also SEARCH DIRECTORY.

discussion board

Discussion boards (also known as bulletin boards, newsgroups, forums, and discussion groups) are published on a website, and allow people to read all the messages left by other people on a particular topic and post new or follow-up messages. Discussion boards are more casual than email mailing lists, as the reader can read what's being discussed without having to subscribe.

An effective adaptation of the discussion board approach is Amazon.com's method for handling reader book reviews. After reading a particular book, a visitor to the site can then write a review of that book, and so help other would-be purchasers.

A discussion board should be moderated. The moderator should keep the contributions on the topic, and discourage personal attacks (it's a good idea to discourage anonymity for this reason). Inform contributors of the privacy policy, give them contact details, and tell them to keep it legal.

See EMAIL MAILING LIST, MODERATOR, ONLINE COMMUNITY.

disk

In relation to computer science, this is always spelled with a *k*.

diskette

Refer to this as a floppy disk, or disk, instead.

DNS

Stands for Domain Name System, the system by which domain names (for example, www.microsoft.com) are translated into IP addresses (for example, 194.12.13.12).

document

A self-contained unit of content. A document is generally made up of text, although it may also include graphics, tables, and/or forms.

document layout

See WEBSITE LAYOUT AND DESIGN.

document navigation

This is navigation that occurs within a document by making a word or short sentence into a link. Avoid linking an entire sentence, unless the sentence is very short.

Choose a set of words that will be as self-explanatory as possible, making the link read like a heading. Avoid creating too many links within a particular document. Only link to what is genuinely relevant. Remember, a link is an invitation to the reader to leave the document.

An alternative way of dealing with links within a document is to place them in a list at the end of the document, or in the right column beside the document.

Avoid linking repeatedly to the same source. Link only the first time you mention the source. For example, if the document frequently mentions Intel, just link to Intel the first time you mention it. See also NAVIGATION.

document templates

Metadata, whether it is XML-based or not, needs to be collected through what are called "document templates." Document templates allow for the collection of the metadata for a particular document type in a structured and repeatable manner. Most organizations will have a small number of document template types. For example, in the financial industry, there would be "morning note" templates, "industry report" templates, and so on.

When creating document templates, remember to keep the number of fields small to avoid making the contribution process more convoluted. In addition, give the template a straightforward name, such as "Morning Note," so that the contributor will quickly recognize it. See Figure 3.3.

domain name

A domain name is an address of a network connection organized in a hierarchical system with each label separated by a dot. Most domain names take the form of "server.organization.type," with non-US domain names taking the form "server.organization.country."

www.yahoo.com (US)

www.yahoo.co.uk (UK)

FIGURE 3.3

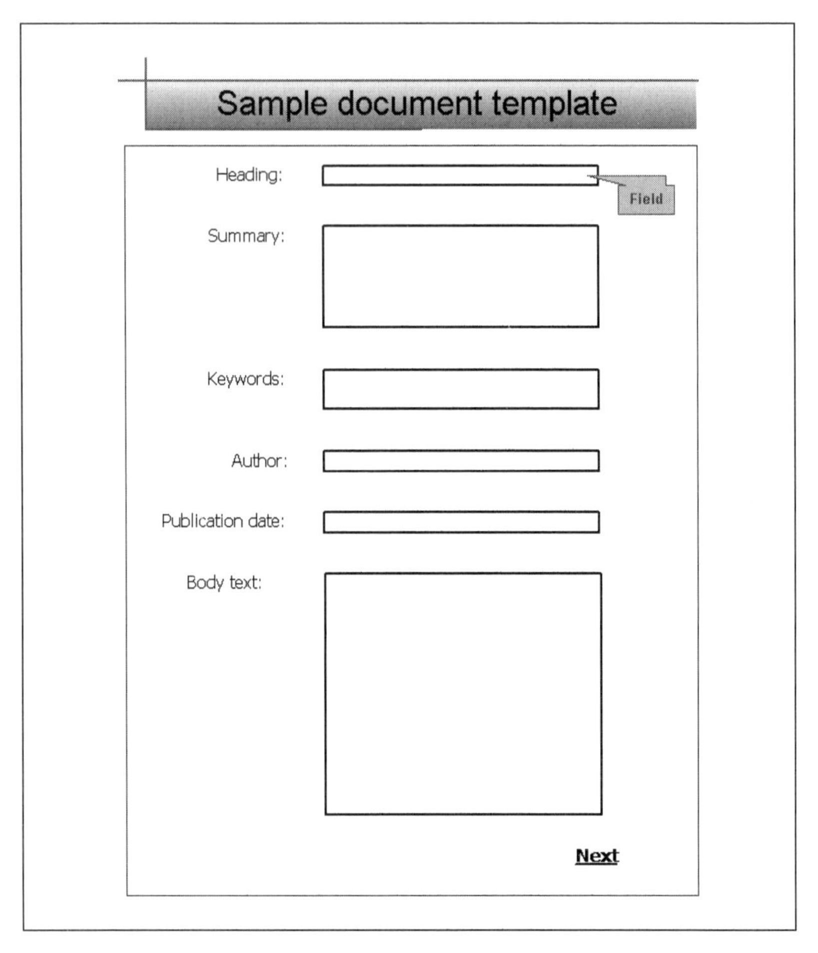

All fields must be filled in, ensuring all the necessary metadata is collected. The next page would then collect information on the classification, and so on.

dotcom

Generally refers to a website intended for commercial use (especially those that do not have an offline business), but is often used to refer to any Web-related company. See also PURE-PLAY.

double opt-in

This requires that a person who has agreed to something (being added to an email mailing list, for example) be sent a verification message by email that they must respond to before the action takes effect. This ensures that readers understand what they're agreeing to, and it prevents third parties from subscribing people to email lists without their knowledge. The double opt-in approach is recommended, particularly from an email marketing point of view. See also EMAIL MARKETING, VERIFICATION MESSAGE.

download times

See PAGE DOWNLOADS.

downtime

A system is "down" when it is not available to readers. Downtime can include time lost because the system has crashed, or because it has been made temporarily unavailable to readers while critical maintenance is being carried out. Planned downtime should be kept to an absolute minimum and should occur at the quietest time of the day for the website. See also CRASH.

drill down

Two words as a verb.

drop-down

Hyphenated as an adjective:

> You can select your name from the drop-down box provided.

drop-down navigation

This is navigation delivered by a drop-down menu. Drop-down navigation is becoming popular as a way of expanding the options provided by the global, core, or language and geographic navigation. It's normally used as a space-saving device and to avoid too much clutter. It shouldn't be used to replace the traditional presentation of navigation in a linear or horizontal format, but rather to supplement and expand on these formats. It can also be used to present an entire lower level of a classification tree. See Figure 3.4.

FIGURE 3.4

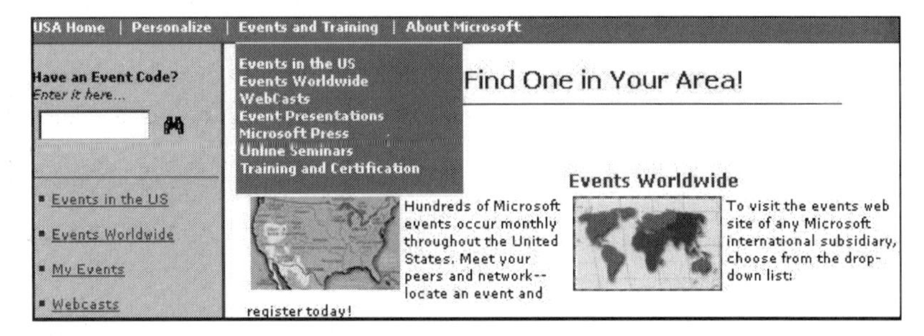

An example of drop-down navigation from Microsoft.com

The reader should be sent to the selection immediately after they select from the drop-down. If they are, there is no need for a 'Go' button beside it, as it may only confuse them. The only circumstance in which you might need it is if you are providing support for older browsers that don't send the reader to the selection automatically.

See also NAVIGATION.

DSL

Stands for digital subscriber line, the general term for a type of high-speed, high-capacity Internet connection that uses traditional copper phone lines. The speed and quality of the connection deteriorates the further a subscriber is from a local telephone exchange. See also ADSL.

DTP

Stands for desktop publishing, the use of a computer and specialized software to combine text and graphics to create a document ready to be published. Most DTP files can be converted to PDF format for Web publication, but this should be done with caution. See also PDF.

dumb down

Meaning simply, with a strong connotation of oversimplify, it is often used in a sneering way by the technology elite. Simplicity is not dumbing down—for years, America Online (AOL) was ridiculed by such an elite because it "dumbed down" its services for average Americans. What AOL did was to keep it simple—like the vast majority of successful websites.

DVD

Stands for digital video disk. DVDs can store much more than a conventional CD-ROM, up to 4.7 GB of data. Also called digital versatile disk.

Dynamic HTML

See DHTML.

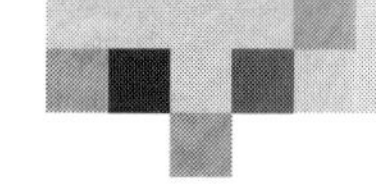

E

e

The most used and abused letter on the Internet. There is much discussion about whether to accept or reject the plethora of words that have been coined by adding e to an existing word. Whether you decide to use all or only some of these new words is a decision for your editors to make and incorporate into your style guide. We recommend that if a word is in common usage, use it; if it's not, don't. The world of Web language is an ever-changing one and it's a careful balancing act to get the right mix between allowing for its changing nature and being a stickler for "traditional" language.

Likewise, whether to hyphenate words beginning with e is also a controversial (in editing circles at any rate) area. At the moment, the unhyphenated form seems to be gaining ground over the hyphenated version—take *email* as an example. There are valid usage arguments for retaining the hyphen, but like the *Oxford English Dictionary*, we take a descriptive rather than a proscriptive approach to language. As always, decide on the spelling you will use, add it to your style guide, and apply it consistently.

ebook

Electronic book.

ebusiness

Business conducted over the Internet. See also B2B.

ecommerce

Any sales conducted over the Internet, but increasingly used to refer to retail sales to consumers. See B2C.

ecommerce/shopping-cart navigation

Ecommerce or shopping-cart navigation allows the reader to move through a purchase process. Key links in this navigation should be presented in a prominent position on every page, generally near the top of the page, or in the masthead (see Figure 3.5). Ecommerce navigation will include links such as: "Shopping cart," "Account," "Help."

FIGURE 3.5

Amazon ecommerce navigation links can be found on the top right of its masthead.

A number of surveys have shown that an alarming number of people fail to complete purchase processes on websites, a key reason being because people find the process too complicated and/or too long. The need to simplify the ecommerce purchase navigation cannot be overemphasized.

When designing ecommerce navigation, ask only for the information that is vital to complete the purchase, and test, test, test.

See also NAVIGATION.

EDI

Stands for Electronic Data Interchange, the electronic communication of business documents or other data between companies. Increasingly, Internet ebusiness systems are replacing traditional EDI systems.

editing content

Editing is about preparing content for publication. It is an essential quality control function. Editing is about making sure that the good stuff gets published and the bad stuff doesn't. It's about making sure that what is published reflects the publication scope, the key messages, the agreed style and tone, etc. Good editing makes for a good publication; poor editing makes for a bad one.

Poor editing is becoming an unfortunate hallmark of Web content. A car manufacturer would never allow a new car off a production line covered in scratches, yet content is published every day on the Web littered with grammatical and punctuation mistakes. The result is that people are becoming increasingly skeptical about Web content. A major Forrester Research survey in 2000 found that 75 percent of respondents believed content on the Web was of a poor quality.

Essential steps in the editing process involve ensuring the quality of the content; checking style and tone; checking for accuracy; checking for grammatical and spelling errors; and checking the metadata. Always check the text in a good word processing program with spell-checking and search features before it is transferred to HTML. See EDITOR, FACT CHECKING, METADATA.

editor

The editor has broad authority for the nature and quality of content. Editors should be empowered to commission content from writers (or to acquire it from third parties), and should have wide latitude in deciding basic questions of length, tone, and completeness. The editor determines whether a given piece of content must be rewritten, and must be able to rearrange and rewrite the content if needs be.

editorial board

A group of designated individuals that oversees and reviews the editorial policy of a website, usually within a large or complex organization. An editorial board should include representatives from all the organization's key constituencies. A large corporation with an intranet, for instance, would at a minimum want an editorial board that included representatives from the company's operating units, marketing, human resources, legal, and finance.

e.g., i.e., etc.

Don't overuse abbreviations such as e.g., i.e., or etc. Use "for example," "for instance," "in other words," "that is," "and so on," "and so forth" instead. See also ET CETERA.

egovernment

Short for electronic government, making government and state-related information, services, and forms available online. Can extend to include online voting.

elearning

One word.

electronic wallet

Software for ecommerce payments containing customers' billing and shipping details, and a digital encryption certificate. Also known as a digital wallet.

ellipsis (...)

An ellipsis (three dots) may be used to indicate either a pause in speaking or an omission of one or more words in a quoted passage. If something is left out *between* sentences, you have two options: use a period to complete the sentence and follow that with the ellipsis, making four dots altogether, or standardize on three dots whether the sentence is finished or not. Decide on your style and add it your STYLE GUIDE. There should be a space before and after the ellipsis.

"Sigh no more, ladies ... men were deceivers ever."

em dash (—)

See DASH.

email

One word, see also E.

email addresses

Email addresses are not case sensitive. Type all email addresses in lowercase for consistency and to help the reader.

email mailing list

An email mailing list is a system that allows you to create, manage, and control the flow of email-based content between a group of readers. Messages sent to the group can be read by all those who have subscribed to the mailing list. Mailing lists allow for the exploration of complex ideas over a period of time, and can become a channel for positive ideas for the organization in relation to improving its products and services.

The best way to explain the benefits of a mailing list is through an example. Let's say you want to get a discussion going with regard to the future direction of a product. You could establish a mailing list, select a moderator, and invite contributions. People on the list would contribute their ideas by email. These emails would go to the moderator who would judge their quality. Depending on the publication schedule, the moderator would send out a digest of the best contributions. This digest would hopefully spark more ideas and more contributions. The mailing list gets a life of its own as product ideas and features are discussed and explored.

When running a mailing list, moderate if at all possible; send a welcome/confirmation email message to new subscribers; clearly state the mailing list's aims; seed the list with interesting content that will provoke discussion; provide the email address for contributions as well as a contact address for technical questions; and give information on how to subscribe to and unsubscribe from the list.

See also MODERATOR, OPT-IN, DOUBLE OPT-IN.

email marketing

Email marketing is a proven way of attracting and keeping customers, and is a perfect complement to a website in that a website is a pull medium (the consumer must actively decide to go to the website) whereas email is a push medium (the content is sent directly to the consumer).

A key issue to address in email marketing is that the consumer has agreed or "opted-in" to receive the email marketing communication. Otherwise the email is considered spam. Opting in requires the consumer's consent. Double opt-in is becoming the convention.

Email marketing communications can be occasional or in the form of a regular email newsletter. The drawback with email marketing is that everybody is now doing it, and so many people are suffering from email overload, and are deleting all but the essential emails they receive. It is thus crucial that your email is of genuine relevance to the receiver. See EMAIL NEWSLETTER, DOUBLE OPT-IN, OPT-IN, SPAM.

email newsletter

An email newsletter (publication) is a collection of content, generally laid out in plain-text format, delivered to a subscriber base on a regular basis. Email newsletters are a highly effective and economic way of delivering content, establishing customer loyalty, and building your brand. They should be a priority of any website publication.

- **Establishing an email newsletter:** Isolate a need within the target readership for the regular delivery of a specific type of content that matches organizational objectives. Agree the regularity of publication. How often will your reader want this content? Generally, once a week, or even once a month, tends to be good for email publications. Whatever the regularity, it is essential that you adhere to the publication schedule.

  Agree the length of the newsletter. Email publications should be short. If necessary, summarize content and put a link back to the full document on the website. Agree the minimum amount of information that needs to be gathered for a reader to subscribe. The longer the subscription form, the less likely it is that the reader will subscribe. Gather only the information that you really need.

  Make a clear distinction between editorial content and advertising. Always build your subscription base on an opt-in basis. Otherwise, you are spamming your readership. See SUBSCRIPTION-BASED PUBLISHING, OPT-IN, DOUBLE OPT-IN, SPAM.

- **General standards:** Use plain text. The best font to use is a non-proportional font such as Courier because it will remain constant in different email packages. The line character length should be no more than 70 characters across, as a number of email management systems break up lines longer than that. Unless it's an exceptional circumstance, never send an attachment as part of an email publication.

- **Subject line:** In a news-oriented newsletter, the subject line should contain the title of the newsletter first, then the date. In an opinion piece newsletter, the subject line should contain the title of the newsletter first, then the title of the piece.

- **Using hypertext:** Use hypertext liberally within your email publication with the objective of getting the reader to visit your website for further information. When creating a hyperlink/URL within an email publication, always use the full address (http://www.) as some email systems will not turn it into a link otherwise. When dealing with a long URL (over 65 characters) put angle brackets (< >) at the beginning and the end of the URL. Otherwise, it may get broken up by the email system and become unusable. When dealing with an email address, use the mailto: function in front of the email address. For example, mailto:tom@xyz.com.

- **Laying out advertising text:** Advertising text should be clearly differentiated from the rest of the content by the use of a border above and below it (for example, "*************"). Try to keep advertisements short (maximum five lines) and make sure they have an email or URL included.
- **Laying out editorials:** As you cannot use font size to differentiate the heading from the body of the text, it is useful to use "all caps" for the heading (for example, TECH STOCKS SLUMP). In general, it is better to identify the author of a particular article as this makes the reader more comfortable. Keep paragraphs short.
- **HTML email newsletters:** There is a trend to create email newsletters in HTML format, which essentially allows what looks like a Webpage to be delivered by email. An HTML newsletter definitely delivers more impact and is more suitable for a consumer-driven sell, where you want readers to click a link in the newsletter and go to the website to buy something.

  However, some older email software programs do not support HTML. Also, HTML newsletters are larger in file size than plain text, and some readers may not want to take the time to download them. If you are distributing an HTML newsletter, offer a version in plain text as well.
- **Other necessary information:** Insert a link to the publication on the Web. Describe the privacy policy in relation to how subscribers' personal information will be used. Link to the full privacy policy on the website. Explain copyright issues relating to the publication. Give clear subscription and unsubscription details. Remind the subscriber to unsubscribe using the *exact* email address they subscribed with, as this is a common mistake (if possible, include this original email subscription information in the newsletter). Give an email contact for technical or other problems the subscriber may encounter. A telephone contact is also helpful.

email signature

An email signature is the text that appears at the bottom of every email someone sends, usually containing essential information on the sender and the organization they work for. Email signatures should be kept short, with a maximum of five lines of text. A long signature is particularly annoying when someone is contributing to an email mailing list, as they make the publication overly long.

Email signatures are a good way to promote the content on your website. Employees send a lot of emails every day and if a short promotion is put in each signature, it can deliver a lot of exposure. The promotion should always contain a URL and/or email address. (Remember to use the full URL including "http://" as partial URLs are not turned into clickable links by some email programs. Also, use a "mailto:" for email addresses.)

email to a friend

A viral marketing website facility that allows readers to interact with other readers by allowing them to easily email information to another person on a document they have just read. See also VIRAL MARKETING.

email writing

Writing emails, like writing other content on the Web, is all about being brief and to the point. (There are billions of emails sent every day!) Treat the subject line as you would a heading for a document. It needs to be short, descriptive, and punchy. If it's not, the reader may not bother opening the email.

While writing style is more casual with emails, particularly between co-workers, make a reasonable attempt to correct spelling mistakes and poor grammar. Some emails looks like a mangled car crash of words. As a rule, address the person you're emailing and end the email with your name.

If something really annoys you, don't rush off an email. Count to 10, at least. If you receive a long email, and your reply is "Yes," don't reply with all the original text you received. Cut it. Send emails when you have something valuable to say. Avoid using the "cc" function just for the sake of it—there's enough email overload. Never write anything in an email that you're not prepared to hear read out in a litigation court.

emarketplaces

Business websites that reduce inefficiencies in markets by allowing buyers and suppliers to trade more efficiently.

emoticon

From the words *emotion* and *icon*, and also known as a *smiley*, an emoticon is an icon composed of letters and symbols that reflects a human facial expression or emotion. For example:

:-) signifies happy

:-(signifies sad

An emoticon gives text more expression and personality. Emoticons are okay to use if you know someone well and it is a personal relationship. However, it is not advisable to use them in commercial communication.

emphasis

See SPECIAL TREATMENT OF WORDS.

encryption

The process of encoding data to prevent unauthorized access, especially during transmission. It requires a key for decoding.

en dash (–)

See DASH.

end user, end-user

Two words as a noun, hyphenated as an adjective. The person who uses a computer or computer application in its finished, marketable form.

error messages

You need to create error messages for times when the website is having technical difficulties or the reader has incorrectly filled in a form or made a wrong selection. When developing error messages, make sure the displayed error is written in a friendly tone in plain English, and not some technical mumbo jumbo. Make sure it's specific—if the reader has filled out a 30-field form, don't just tell them that they haven't filled out the form correctly, inform them of the exact section in which they made an error. For example, the message should *not* say: "Some fields in your form were not filled out correctly." Rather, it *should* say: "It seems that your email address has not been entered correctly."

etailer

Online retailer of consumer goods or services.

et cetera, etc.

Formal writing discourages the use of *et cetera* and its abbreviation *etc.* Although the Web tends to be less formal than traditional publishing, you should still avoid overusing this as it can often simply look lazy. The abbreviated form, *etc.*, should always take a period and both forms should be preceded by a comma.

> They played football, tennis, squash, etc.

It is also followed by a comma, unless it is the final element in a series, in which case the inclusion of the comma is dependent on what grammar dictates, or if it appears at the end of a sentence:

> The man's hat, coat, bag, etc. were filthy.
>
> The man's hat, coat, bag, etc., not to mention his hands, were filthy.

Ethernet

This is the most widely installed local area network (LAN). Ethernet was originally developed by Xerox in 1976 and then developed further by Xerox, DEC, and Intel.

European currency

See FOREIGN CURRENCIES.

exabyte

1,152,921,504,606,846,976 bytes (1,024 petabytes).

extension

See FILE EXTENSION.

extranet

A password-protected website for a company's customers, which is not available to the general public. Apply the same standards to an extranet as you apply to an Internet website. Remember, the most important reader of all is looking at the extranet—your customer!

ezine

Electronic magazine available on the Internet, usually free of charge.

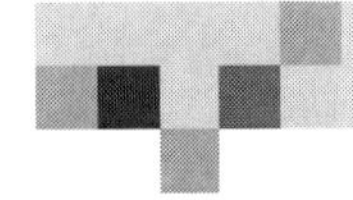

F

fact checking

Before content is published, and after it's been edited, it should be fact-checked. Often, in the course of writing, revising, and editing content, numbers, dates, names, and quotes can be entered incorrectly or changed during the editing process in subtle but meaningful ways. The best way to rid content of such errors is to check each fact methodically once the content is in final, about-to-be-published form.

The best way to fact-check content is to print out the text, read it line by line, and make a physical checkmark next to every verifiable fact after comparing it with an original source. The fact-checkers (often the writers) should force themselves to do this even when they are sure that the copy is right. This requires a mental switch to an adversarial role: You need to look at each statement and fact and ask questions such as, "Says who?" and, "Is the writer really sure about this?"

If a company or other organization is named, for instance, check the organization's website to make sure the name is correctly spelled and punctuated. The US consumer-goods manufacturer Procter & Gamble, for instance, frequently has its name mangled online and off, with an "and" instead of the ampersand, and with the first word spelled "Proctor" rather than "Procter."

If the organization has no website, a printed reference from the company—an annual report, a brochure, or a business card—is the best check. To rely on a secondary source such as a Web article, newspaper, or magazine is to ask for trouble, and risk perpetuating others' mistakes. If secondary sources must be used, you should try to find several, and make sure they agree.

The same degree of care should be taken with names, numbers, titles, and Web addresses. A useful trick with Web addresses is to copy the address and paste it into a browser to see whether it actually goes to the intended website. Another useful piece of simple advice is to always check "millions" and "billions" and make sure you haven't mixed them up.

fall

Lowercase. In British English, *autumn*.

FAQs

Stands for frequently asked questions, a document where the most commonly asked questions from readers are listed along with answers. They are ideal for providing support information and can reduce support demands on your staff.

farewell message

See UNSUBSCRIBE.

favorite

See BOOKMARK.

feature

A feature might be a specific document or general area on the site that you want to promote. Features are a publishing technique. The editor decides what product, service, or event to promote, and then provides the content that can be used as promotion.

Examples of features could be found on most news websites during the 2000 Olympics and the 2001 US presidential election. A major slice of the homepage was allocated to these features, with links and news summaries. After the events, these features were removed from the homepages.

feedback

Feedback is critical to the success of any website. It is vital to know which content is working and which is not, and how the purchase process, search, navigation, forms, and other elements are performing. Without feedback, people could be leaving your website in frustration and you will never know. On the Web, an active strategy for feedback needs to be in place, because unlike the bricks-and-mortar store, customers' reactions and feelings are hard to gauge. To create a well-designed site, you need proper feedback from and usability testing of your readers.

A quality feedback process involves making people aware that their feedback is valued; actively reaching out to the customer, for example by asking them questions when they complete a process; hosting well-moderated discussion boards or mailing lists; offering prizes or extra services for fully completed feedback forms and participation in focus groups; and replying to people promptly, thanking them, and answering any queries raised in their feedback.

fewer, less

Fewer should be used with something that can be counted and is used with plural nouns. *Less* refers to degree or amount—something measurable but not countable, such as *effort*—and is used with singular nouns.

Fewer accidents were reported.

Less effort was required.

file extension

The tag used to identify a file, usually a period followed by between two and four letters. When referring to a particular file extension, show the extension in lowercase, preceded by a period, for example

Microsoft Word files are indicated by the .doc extension.

When referring to files in general by their extension types, use uppercase and don't precede the extension with a period, for example

You will need Adobe Acrobat Reader to read PDF files.

File Transfer Protocol

See FTP.

filename

One word.

file-naming conventions

To help the successful organization of your site, you should ensure that files are named consistently and correctly.

Filenames should be in lowercase, without gaps (use underscores where names are split), and shouldn't exceed 50 characters. Above all, filenames should be descriptive.

firewall

A firewall is a security system intended to protect an organization's network against unauthorized users.

first, firstly in enumerations

First, second, third in enumerations in American English, *firstly, secondly, thirdly* in British English.

Flash

A technology supplied by Macromedia to generate visually rich animations on the Web. Has become synonymous with over-design. Flash can be very useful where the features of a product need to be demonstrated in a visual way, or where a visual representation of content is much more useful than a text version. However, Flash is greatly abused by designers who don't understand the Web, thinking of it like a TV or glossy magazine medium. It is not.

floppy disk

Also referred to simply as a *floppy*, and less frequently now as a *diskette*.

fonts

Choose sans serif fonts, such as Verdana, Arial, and Univers, if possible, as such fonts use straight lines and are thus easier to read on screen. Serif fonts, on the other hand, use a lot of curves, which tend to read poorly on a screen, particularly at smaller font sizes. Because it's harder to read text on a screen, avoid using small font sizes. Small quantities of text on homepages can be presented as small as 8-point font. However, for body text in a document, you shouldn't use any lower than 10 point.

The font color should be black, except for headings, where a different color can be used. If another font color is used, ensure it's a dark font on a light background. See also COLOR.

footer

A footer contains essential links and information about an organization and should be placed at the bottom of every page of the site. The footer should be clearly separated from the rest of the content on the page through appropriate spacing and/or a line going across the page.

The footer should begin with the global navigation as a set of text links. There are two reasons for this. First, by the time the reader has scrolled down to the end of the page, the global navigation links provided at the top might no longer be visible. Second, global navigation at the top of the page is often in graphical form. Providing a text version improves the accessibility of the page and could improve your listing on a search engine.

See ACCESSIBILITY, SEARCH ENGINE REGISTRATION AND OPTIMIZATION.

Other necessary elements in the footer include ecommerce navigation, if there is ecommerce available; contact information—including email, phone, fax, and physical address (if there are more than two contact points, provide a link to a contact page); a Terms of use link, a privacy policy link, a copyright statement ("Copyright © 1995–2001 Example Company. All rights reserved"), which links to a full copyright statement, if appropriate. See Figure 3.6.

FIGURE 3.6

```
Shopping cart  Checkout  Your account  Help
Home  About  Products  Customers  Support  Contact  Search

Tusade Enterprises, 23 Lee Lane, Hollow Street, Dublin 2, Ireland. Map of location.
Tel: +353 1 456 34 43   Fax: +353 1 456 34 64   Email: info@tusade.com

Privacy policy
Terms of use

Copyright © 1995-2001 Tusade Enterprises. All rights reserved.
```

A sample footer

See TERMS OF USE STATEMENT, PRIVACY POLICY, COPYRIGHT.

foreign currencies

Although many sites originally used only international foreign currency codes (USD) and not money symbols ($) on Webpages, more and more sites are now using money symbols as there is less likelihood that a reader's browser will not be able to display them. Whichever you choose, apply it consistently.

For plain-text formats, such as email, use the foreign currency code, not the symbol:

Daily online sales pass $200 million for first time. [Webpage]

Daily online sales pass USD 200 million for first time. [email]

For symbols, you can use the $ symbol on its own if it's clear that it's for the US dollar, but identify all other types of dollar, for example CAN$, etc. (If, however, the site is an intranet for an Australian company with only Australian-based employees, for example, then the use of the $ symbol on its own to mean an Australian dollar would be sufficient as there's no potential for confusion.)

The following European Union member states have adopted the common European currency (the euro): Belgium, Germany, Greece, Spain, France, Ireland, Italy, Luxembourg, the Netherlands, Austria, Portugal, and Finland. Initially, provide amounts for these countries in euros as well as in their own currencies. From 2002, the euro will be the only currency you need to quote for these countries. For updated information, see the European Union website (http://europa.eu.int/euro).

Here are some of the most frequently used currencies, codes, and symbols:

Currency	SYMBOL	CODE
Australian dollar	A$	AUD
Brazil real	R$	BRL
Canadian dollar	Can$	CAD
Chinese yuan	Y	CNY
Danish krone	DKr	DKK
Euro (Austria, Belgium, Finland, France, Germany, Greece, Ireland, Italy, Luxembourg, Netherlands, Portugal, and Spain)	€	EUR
French franc	Fr and €	FRF
German mark	DM and €	DEM
Hong Kong dollar	HK$	HKD

Indian rupee	Re	INR
Indonesian rupiah	Rp	IDR
Irish punt	IR£ and €	IEP
Israeli shekel	I£/ NIS	ILS
Japanese yen	¥	JPY
Mexican peso	Mex$	MXN
New Zealand dollar	NZ$	NZD
Norwegian krone	NKr	NOK
South African rand	R	ZAR
Swedish krona	SKr	SEK
Swiss franc	Sw F	CHF
UK pound (sterling)	£	GBP
US dollar	$ [US$]	USD

For a full list, see the Foreign Money section in the *United States Government Printing Office Style Manual* available online at www.access.gpo.gov/styleman/2000/browse-sm-00.html

formats

Avoid using non-standard technologies that require viewing with either plug-ins or stand-alone applications as they can cause accessibility problems. When inaccessible technologies must be used, provide equivalent accessible pages if possible.

If the reader clicks a link, they expect to go to an HTML page. If it's a non-HTML page, inform them in advance. Tell them they are linking to an audio file, PDF, etc., and inform them of the size of that file. Provide a link to a copy of the necessary software if available online. See also ACCESSIBILITY.

formatting

Italics can be hard to read on screen and therefore should be avoided in general text, particularly when used in conjunction with small fonts. Bold (particularly colored bold) can be mistaken for a link. Underlining *will* be taken for a link. See the entries under ITALICS and BOLD for more information on this, including when to use either.

Use regular font (not bold, not italics) in quotation marks for article titles, report titles, chapter titles, and shorter poems. Use regular font for website names:

You can find the information on FT.com.

forms

Forms are used to collect information from a reader in a structured manner that ensures all essential information is collected. For example, when someone is subscribing to a service on a website, they should be asked to fill in a form, which will request, among other things, their email address.

With a form, the email address is hidden. Therefore you should also use forms for contact information because you can collect specific information and it prevents spammers from collecting (harvesting) your email addresses with special software.

- **Keep forms short:** We all hate filling out forms. It's a fact of life. So, keep every form as short and as simple as possible. Collect only essential information. If your form is long, break it up into a number of pages to avoid putting off the reader.
- **Opinion questions first:** Readers are more open to giving their opinion, so place the opinion-type questions up front and ask the demographic-type questions toward the end of the form.
- **Mandatory fields:** Clearly mark the mandatory fields by way of font color or use of asterisks, and inform the reader what signifies a mandatory field. Be careful not to mandate information that certain readers cannot provide. For example, if the form is to be filled out by an international readership, don't make a ZIP code obligatory.
- **Errors:** The process should check for obvious errors. For example, if the email address input has more than three characters at its end it's likely to be a mistake—mary@abcd.comm, the final "m" being a mistake. We all make errors when filling out forms, and it's very frustrating to have the entire form returned to hunt for the error. Isolate the error

for the reader if possible. For example, if the reader forgot to fill out their email address, inform them:

> Your email address has not been filled out. Please go back and fill it out.

- **Answer field size:** Ensure the answer field has enough room in it for the input being asked. For example, don't have a small field when asking for address information, as some people have quite long addresses. Arial is the recommended font for forms, as it is a narrow font, thus allowing the maximum number of characters to be input into the minimum space.
- **Accessibility:** Allow people using assistive technology to access all the information, field elements, and functionality required for completion and submission of the form, including all directions and cues.
- **Test:** Test your forms regularly with dummy data to make sure they are working properly.

See also HARVEST.

forums

See DISCUSSION BOARD.

forward, forwards

Forward in American English, *forwards* in British English.

forward slash (/)

Also known as an oblique stroke or a solidus, the forward slash is sometimes used to indicate a period extending over two calendar years. It can also be used to indicate alternatives. Place no spacing either side of the slash:

> 1998/9
> and/or

See also DATES.

fractions

Hyphens are used when fractions are expressed in words:

> two-thirds of the respondents

A mixed number is not spelled out:

> 2½, *not* two and a half

frames

Frames break up a Webpage into two or more distinct sections. It's like having a website within a website. In the words of usability design expert Jakob Nielsen. "Frames: Just Say No."

Netscape invented frames, and within days the entire Netscape website was using frames. There was so much negative reader feedback that within weeks the Netscape website got rid of its frames. It never used them again.

What's so wrong with frames? Well, they can cause problems with bookmarking, the Back button, and printing. They are more likely to have buggy code due to their level of technical difficulty. Search engines often get confused trying to index frames-based websites. They tend to take longer to download, and they can create accessibility problems. Need we go on?

So, is there ever a time when frames make sense? Yes. When it is of fundamental importance that a piece of navigation is kept permanently on the screen.

If you insist on using frames, ensure each frame is titled in order to facilitate navigation and frame identification, and provide a non-framed version also.

See also ACCESSIBILITY.

freeware

Software that is free to use. Internet Explorer and Netscape Navigator are examples of freeware.

frequency

See PUBLICATION SCHEDULE.

front end, front-end

Two words as a noun (the front end), hyphenated as an adjective (front-end software). The front end is the part of an application that users interact with. See also BACK END.

FTP

Stands for File Transfer Protocol, a basic Internet protocol used for copying files to and from computer systems.

full stop

The British English word for a period. See PERIOD.

gateway

A device that connects networks using different protocols, allowing information exchange.

Gb

See GIGABIT.

GB

See GIGABYTE.

geek

Someone who eats, sleeps, and drinks technology and who lives in the realm of the intellectual, often lacking concern for their physical appearance. Geeks always must have the latest gadget. Sometimes called a nerd—there is a difference between the terms, but it tends to be religious or philosophical rather than practical. See also TECHIE.

geographic navigation

See LANGUAGE AND GEOGRAPHIC NAVIGATION, see also NAVIGATION.

geographic places

Capitalize geographic areas when they are definite geographic places, regions, areas, and countries, for example

> Central America, East Asia, Eastern Europe, Northern Europe, Northern Ireland, Southeast Asia, Southern Europe, The Hague, the Midlands, the Middle East, the Midwest (in the US), the South (in the US), the West, West Coast (of the US), Western Europe

However, their adjectives can be lowercase:

> Faulkner was a southern writer.

Use lowercase for province, county, state, and city, when not strictly part of the name:

> Washington state, New York city

Use lowercase for east, west, north, south, except when part of a name (South Africa).

getting linked

When other websites link to yours it's like embedded word of mouth and is a powerful means of promoting content. Alexa.com gives information on how many links a website has.

Another website will link to you only if it feels that you have valuable content that its readers want. The easiest way to get links is to offer reciprocal linking. Ideally, however, you want to get as many websites as possible to link to you without having to link back to them. The stronger your content is, the more chance you have of getting websites to link to you. However, having quality content is not enough. You need to allocate staff to contact targeted websites and propose they link to you.

Remember, getting linked is a slow process, but it is well worth it in the long run.

See also PROMOTING CONTENT.

GIF

Stands for graphic interchange format, a compression format for images, particularly common on the Internet for non-photographic images. See GRAPHICS.

gigabit

1,073,741,824 bits, abbreviated Gb.

gigabyte

1,073,714,824 bytes (1,024 megabytes), abbreviated GB.

global navigation

Global navigation contains links to pages that must be accessible from every page on the site. Such links include the key sections of content that the organization has to offer (Products, Services, Support, etc.). Global navigation should be placed at the top and bottom of every page. In smaller websites, where there is no core navigation, the global navigation is often found near the top of the page in the left column.

Global navigation acts as an anchor point for the reader. It's how they easily get back to central parts of the website. Thus, once agreed on, it should not be changed, except for very good reasons. The regular reader of the website will have become used to it and will be confused by such changes.

Global navigation should always be viewable from the first screen. Ideally, it should be near the top of the screen, and should be integrated into the masthead. (See MASTHEAD.) The global navigation should always start with a "Home" link. It is highly recommended to also have "Contact" and "About" links.

If the website is a sub-site of a larger website, then a link to the homepage of the larger website needs to be considered. For example: "microsoft.com Home," "Office Home." These links should be clearly separated to avoid confusion.

Global navigation should not have more than eight links. If a global navigation is to have more than eight links, it is highly recommended to break it into two sections. The first section should deal with essential "housekeeping" links, such as Home, Contact, Help, and so on. The second section should deal with more marketing-driven links such as Products, Services, Solutions, Support, and so on. The second section should contain a "Home" link for the product or product group, such as "Office Home."

It is recommended that the marketing-driven global navigation is in a larger size font than the housekeeping global navigation, as it is a more important navigation to present to the reader.

Where there is a relatively small quantity of content on the website, it may suffice to have only a global navigation on the homepage. In other words, there is no need for CORE NAVIGATION.

For design reasons, the global navigation may appear as a graphic at the top of the page. It should also be presented as text links in the footer. This is important from an accessibility and search engine optimization point of view. See Figure 3.7.

FIGURE 3.7

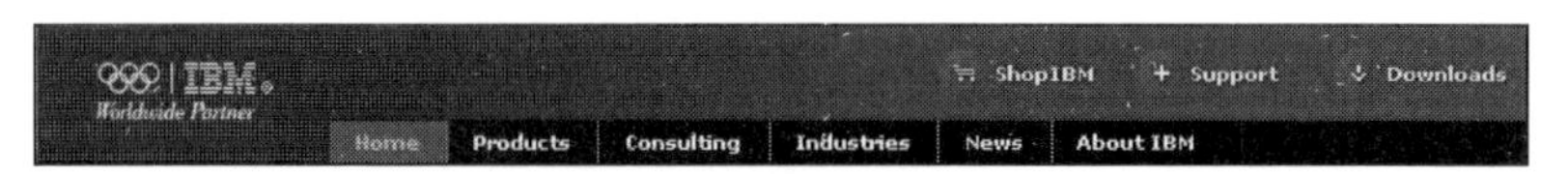

An example of the IBM global navigation

See also CORE NAVIGATION, NAVIGATION, ACCESSIBILITY, SEARCH ENGINE REGISTRATION AND OPTIMIZATION.

glossary

See STYLE GUIDE.

Gnutella

This is a peer-to-peer file-sharing network that allows Internet users to swap any sort of file without having to go through a central server.

government

See COLLECTIVE NOUNS.

GPRS

Stands for General Packet Radio Service, an enhancement to the GSM wireless system that supports the transfer of data packets, thus speeding up activities such as Web browsing and file transfer.

graphics

A picture may indeed say a thousand words, but on the Web that same picture might also take up 1,000 KB. Compare that with the 5 KB that 1,000 words of perfect English take up. GIFs and JPEGs allow smaller file sizes, but at the cost of quality. Until we reach broadband nirvana (circa 2005 or later), minimal use of graphics is advised.

On the homepage, all logos and associated graphics should be kept to a minimum size (preferably 7 KB) and should link to the story they are related to, if any. If you believe the reader might wish to see a larger version of the graphic, provide a small version, with a link to a larger version. Inform the reader of the size of the larger version. For example: "Click here for larger version (20 KB)."

All images should have associated "ALT" text. This is helpful, as the information can be read before the graphic downloads, and it also supports readers who have switched off graphics in their browser. The ALT tag is also essential for readers with visual impairments.

In general, avoid animating graphics. If it is animated, give the reader the choice to stop/start the animation. Alternatively, it can animate just once and then stop.

For pictures, save as .jpeg. For other graphics, save as .gif. See also ACCESSIBILITY, ALT TEXT.

graphics within documents

A graphic should usually be right-aligned or horizontal across the column (left-aligned can cause accessibility problems). A good place for them to appear is at the top of the document, underneath the heading. A graphic should not dominate the screen.

If the graphic's copyright is different from the document's, the copyright information should appear before the descriptive text. If the copyright notice is already embedded in the graphic, there's no need to repeat the information.

Follow the normal rules for graphics. See GRAPHICS, WEBSITE LAYOUT AND DESIGN.

GSM

Stands for Global System for Mobile Communications, the standard digital wireless technology in Europe and Asia.

GUI

Stands for graphical user interface, and pronounced "gooey," an environment that represents programs, files, and options by means of icons, menus, and dialog boxes on the screen, which was popularized by the Mac in the 1980s.

GUI widgets

Ensure you use GUI widgets, such as radio buttons and checkboxes, as readers have come to expect. For example, a reader should be able to select only *one* radio button, whereas they can select multiple checkboxes. Books such as *Microsoft Windows User Experience* (published by the Microsoft Press in 1999) will help you with this.

hacker

Originally used to refer to someone who likes to examine computer program and operating codes, hacker is now commonly accepted to mean anyone who breaks into computer systems without the permission of the owner.

hang

This occurs when a computer stops responding or "crashes." See CRASH.

harvest

The process by which spammers use specially designed software to collect email addresses from websites. The objective is to add these email addresses to a spam database, then sell that database to other spammers, or send out spam emails to that database. A way of avoiding having your email addresses harvested is to use email forms. See also FORMS, SPAM.

he/she

See SEXIST LANGUAGE.

heading and summary

See WEBSITE LAYOUT AND DESIGN.

headings

Headings (also known as headlines) on the Web serve several functions. In addition to telling the reader what the content is about and enticing them to read on, they are often the way that readers find your content in the first place. They are the first words picked up by search engines, and are sometimes the only text about your article that will show up in search engine results. Your headings should be short, direct, and utilitarian. They should describe the content succinctly and include as many keywords as possible. For examples and tips on writing headings, see page 5.

headlines

See HEADINGS.

high-tech (adjective)

We'd recommend against using the variant of this, *hi-tech*.

historical periods

See AGES/PERIODS OF HISTORY.

history trail

See CLASSIFICATION PATH NAVIGATION.

hit

Every time a single item, such as a text file, is requested from a Web server, it is counted as a hit. Hits are a horrific abuse of statistics and a totally unreliable indicator of traffic to a website. It's like this—every time a single Webpage, built up of many files, is requested from the server, as many as 20 hits might be counted. Saying that your website had 1,000 hits is thus a totally unreliable, inflated way to measure how many people visited your website, or how many pages they viewed.

The industry standard for website measurement is now page views/impressions, visitors, and unique visitors. It is usually safe to divide the number of hits by 10 to get the number of page views. So, 1,000 hits to a website would equate to 100 page views. See PAGE VIEW, VISITOR.

homepage

The first page of a website. There are also sub-homepages, which are the first pages for major sections within the website. There should be a link to the homepage on every page on the site. This link should be titled "Home." The default homepage is the page that the browser goes to when it is opened.

A homepage should promote key content and upcoming events, allow visitors to quickly find what they are looking for, and tell the visitor what your company does.

See DEFAULT HOMEPAGE, WEBSITE LAYOUT AND DESIGN, PROMOTING CONTENT.

homepage design

See WEBSITE LAYOUT AND DESIGN.

homepage navigation

A primary function of a homepage is to provide context for the reader. Homepage navigation is not simply about functional navigation such as classifications and search. It also takes out content highlights from the content archive, presenting them as summaries and/or features. See also WEBSITE LAYOUT AND DESIGN.

homepage promotion

See PROMOTING CONTENT.

host

This is the computer on which a website is physically located.

hotspot

One word—the exact clickable area on screen that will be affected when a mouse pointer is held over it. On a Webpage this area is usually a section of text, an icon, image, or button with an embedded link.

HTML

Stands for Hypertext Markup Language, the markup language used to build documents on the Web.

HTTP

Stands for Hypertext Transfer Protocol, the basic Internet protocol that allows Web servers and browsers to send and receive information on the Web.

hyperlinks

See LINKS.

hypermedia

An environment that links not just text but other media such as video, animation, and audio.

hypertext

Hypertext is text that is linked. It allows a reader to move from one document to another simply by clicking. While print text is linear, hypertext can have multiple paths that lead in multiple directions. Many people believe that hypertext better reflects how the mind works—by association. Hypertext is the main concept behind the invention of the Web—it's what allows such a vast amount of information to be linked together.

Hypertext allows you to create content in a pyramid structure, with a short heading or summary at the top, and then as the reader clicks down, longer and more detailed content. This approach maps the behavior of the reader, because as they click deeper into a content area, their interest in the subject is obviously heightened and they are moving from a scan read to a more detail-focused read. It also allows you to link between documents, enabling the reader to quickly find further reading on a particular subject.

hyphens

Hyphens are often necessary for clarity or convention. But don't overuse them. It is a good idea to add frequently queried compound words and adjectives, as well as prefixes, to your style guide.

- **Compound words:** Related words (compounds) have three degrees of intimacy—they can be written as two separate words (salad dressing), joined by hyphens (son-in-law), or written as one word (keyboard).

  For guidance on whether a compound is two words, hyphenated, or one word, you should consult your main reference dictionary. Dictionaries may differ on some entries, which is why it is so important for consistency to nominate one dictionary as the first point of reference for everybody in the organization.

- **Compound adjectives:** Hyphens can clarify the sense when two or more words are used adjectivally before the noun they modify. The hyphen is not normally required when the adjective follows the noun:

  > The room was full of *more important* people. (Ambiguous)

  Here, *more important* is ambiguous—does it refer to "an increase in the number of important people" or "people of greater importance." Change it to

  > The room was full of more-important people. (Not ambiguous)

  When used after the noun, *more important* is not ambiguous:

  > The other people were more important, apparently.

  Adjectives or participles (present or past form of the verb that can serve as an adjective—*spoken* in *well-spoken*) preceded by an adverb are not hyphenated if the adverb ends in *ly* because there is no ambiguity about their meaning:

  > newly married couple

- **Prefixes:** Most standard prefixes do not take hyphens:

unimportant, multicolored

However, many people hyphenate words beginning with *non*, words that are followed by the same vowel as the prefix ending, and words that could be ambiguous without the hyphen:

re-cover (to cover something again)
recover (to regain or restore to a normal state)

Consult your reference dictionary for specific guidelines.

- **Common second element:** Hyphens can be used to represent the common second element in all but the last word of a list:

two-, three-, and fourfold

Use these "hanging hyphens" sparingly—try to rephrase where possible—but whatever you do, don't forget the hyphen:

Incorrect: blue or brown-eyed people (here it is referring to blue people!)

Right: blue- or brown-eyed people

or blue-eyed or brown-eyed people

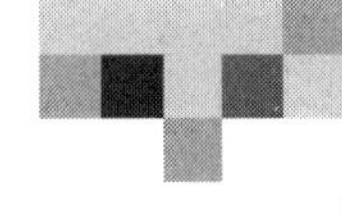

I

ICANN

Stands for Internet Corporation for Assigned Names and Numbers, a private non-profit organization that administers domain name registration and Internet protocols.

icon

Any small onscreen image that represents an object or program. Because of the truly international nature of the Web (a particular icon can mean different things in different cultures), and because of bandwidth and screen size constraints, icons tend to be used sparingly on the Web.

Icons should always have text descriptions (see Figure 3.8). There's no point having a fancy icon that represents "What's New" if a large number of your readers do not recognize it as such. Therefore, put a "What's New" text description underneath or beside the icon. Icons should link to the page they represent (except when they are already on that page, see LINKS).

FIGURE 3.8

Yahoo uses icons with text descriptions underneath.

The rules for GRAPHICS apply to icons also. See GRAPHICS.

ICT

Stands for Information and Communication Technology, the study of the technology used to handle information and aid communication. By adding "Communication" to the more familiar "Information Technology," this term attempts to reflect the increasing role of both information and communication technologies in all aspects of society.

ID

Stands for identification. Use capitals, no periods.

i.e.

See E.G., I.E., ETC.

image map

This is a graphic image that contains more than one link. Clicking different parts of the image links the reader to other resources on another part of the page, a different Webpage, or a file. Try to use client-side rather than server-side image maps for accessibility reasons. See also ACCESSIBILITY, CLIENT SIDE.

i-mode

The interactive wireless information service offered by NTT DoCoMo to Japanese consumers. It is seen as an alternative to WAP, as it has been much more successful in Japan than WAP has been in Europe. See also WAP.

impression

In Web advertising, the term *impression* indicates an advertisement's appearance on a Webpage. Online publishers offer advertising measured in terms of ad views or impressions. If the page you're on shows two ads, that's two impressions, so there will often be more impressions than page impressions.

See also PAGE IMPRESSION.

infomediary

An infomediary (information intermediary) is an organization or individual that collects information on a group of people and then trades that information to gain benefit for that group. For an infomediary to be successful, it must first gain the trust of the group by protecting the privacy of individual members. Then it must have sufficient information on a sufficient number of people to trade profitably, while delivering value to that group.

An example of an infomediary trade would be if the infomediary went to Ford Motor Company and said, "I have 1,000 people who wish to buy cars within the next six months. What discount will I get if they all buy Fords?" If Ford decided to give a special discount, then the infomediary would split that discount between itself and the individual purchasers.

information

Information is the process by which knowledge is communicated. There are two basic methods by which information can be communicated: through person-to-person interaction, and through content.

information age

Term used to differentiate the current era from the industrial era. So called because electronic access to information through computer technology is now a major contributor to Western economies.

information architect

The information architect is responsible for the overall architecture of the website. Specific responsibilities include

- the design and management of the metadata, classification, search, and navigation
- layout and design of the website
- quality of the HTML
- ensuring that pages download quickly
- usability and accessibility
- choice and management of content-management, subscription, logging, and other relevant software

The most important skill an information architect requires is the ability to develop proper metadata designs. Classification design is central here, as is the design of the document templates. Metadata is directly linked to the design of search, and the architect must have an excellent grasp of how to create a search function that is simple to use, yet powerful. Navigation is at the heart of information architecture and the architect must have a keen understanding of navigation design and know when and how to implement various navigation options.

The information architect needs to be skilled in laying out content to achieve optimal readability. This is linked with the "look and feel" of the website, which they should consider with input from the graphic designer. They need to be skilled in HTML and know how to code pages that are fast to download. Information architecture is intertwined with usability and the architect should either have a background in usability design, or should be able to work hand in hand with a usability expert. Among other things, expertise in accessibility design will be required here.

The information architect should have a thorough understanding of the software required to run the publication. They should be able to advise the managing editor on various software options. Their expertise should include

- content-management applications
- subscription-based publishing software
- website-log software
- personalization software
- online-community software (chat, discussion boards, email mailing lists)

See also ACCESSIBILITY, NAVIGATION, WEBSITE LAYOUT AND DESIGN.

information architecture

Information architecture deals with the organization and layout of content on a website. Specifically, it refers to the development of metadata, classification, navigation, search, and content layout.

Good information architecture helps readers to find and read content. It allows them to perform the task they are trying to do in the easiest and most logical manner. It provides appropriate feedback to the reader as they are moving through the website, as well as online help where needed.

See ACCESSIBILITY, INFORMATION ARCHITECT, NAVIGATION, WEBSITE LAYOUT AND DESIGN.

information economy

See NEW ECONOMY.

information literate

In an information economy it is not enough to be able to read and write. For those who want to find quality employment, a new form of literacy is required: information literacy. The International Adult Literacy Survey defines information literacy as "the ability to understand and employ printed information in daily activities, at home, at work, and in the community—to achieve one's goals and to develop one's knowledge and potential." According to the American Library Association: "Ultimately, information-literate people are those who have learned how to learn. They know how to learn because they know how knowledge is organized, how to find information, and how to use information in such a way that others can learn from them."

information overload

Information overload is the modern problem of feeling overwhelmed by information due to the easy access to numerous communications sources filled with vast quantities of content. Because digital content can be reproduced at little cost, the temptation is to produce (or reproduce) that content whether it is useful or not. Information overload is one of the most critical problems individuals and organizations face today.

If you consider that every day there are another 7 million documents added to the 550 billion documents published on the Web, and that over 90 percent of all unique content produced in the world is in digital format, you can get an idea of the scale of the problem. (According to the University of California, Berkeley: "The world's total yearly production of print, film, optical, and magnetic content would require roughly 1.5 billion gigabytes of storage. This is the equivalent of 250 megabytes per person for each man, woman, and child on earth.")

The only workable solution to information overload is better publishing practices. Publishing addresses the core issues such as what to publish and what not to publish. Good publishers will probably reject up to 90 percent of what they receive for publication.

intellectual capital

See KNOWLEDGE CAPITAL.

interactive

Interactive technology is any technology that allows exchange between the user and the computer program. From an Internet perspective, interactivity is the process by which a reader interacts with elements on a website and gets an appropriate response. Interactivity also refers to a situation where a person interacts with other people by communicating through email, discussion boards, chat software, or other tools. Interactivity is always a two-way process. If the organization does not reply to the communication, then no real interactivity has occurred.

interface

The point of connection between two elements that enables them to work with each other.

internal banner advertising

A banner advertising system is a useful tool to promote important content on your site, although it needs to be recognized that banner advertising has significantly diminished in its effectiveness over the past couple of years. See also BANNER AD, PROMOTING CONTENT.

Internet

(Always capitalized, sometimes shortened to Net.) The Internet is a "network of networks." Developed in the 1960s by the US Military—and then called the ARPANET—the Internet became the first system that connected computers regardless of their make or type. Before the Internet, there were only private networks connecting the same types of computers, often in the same building.

The Internet's revolutionary impact is that it allows anyone with a computer, a telephone line, and an Internet service provider (ISP) account to connect up. However, Internet use stayed largely within academia until the invention of the Web by Tim Berners-Lee in the early 1990s. With the Web, Internet use exploded. In 1993, it was estimated that there were roughly 4 million people using the Internet and only 50 websites. By 2000, driven by the Web, this estimate had risen to over 400 million people and perhaps more than 20 million websites. While its two core elements are the Web and email—throughout its history, email has been the most powerful and used tool that the Internet has introduced—Usenet, Telnet, and FTP are also part of the Internet.

Regardless of the hype and the occasional market crash, the Internet is one of the great inventions of mankind. In terms of uptake, it is the fastest growing technology of all time. Truly, the revolution has only begun.

Internet addresses

See WEB ADDRESS.

Internet backbone

The underlying high-speed network connections of the Internet. The backbone carries the heaviest Internet traffic and smaller networks are attached to it.

Internet penetration

This is the level of Internet use in a country or region.

Internet Protocol

See IP.

Internet2

Everyone who uses the Internet recognizes that there is much more that it could achieve if it were faster. For this reason, the Internet2 initiative was launched. Internet2 includes over 180 universities working with industry and government. According to the Internet2 Consortium, the objective is to "develop and deploy advanced network applications and technologies, accelerating the creation of tomorrow's Internet." Basically, Internet2 is about making the Internet much faster.

interstitial

Advertisements that pop up in a new browser window while an Internet reader is waiting for a page to load.

intranet

Lowercase (there is only one Internet; there are many intranets).

An intranet is a publication to staff containing content that helps them to do a better, more efficient job. A quality intranet facilitates staff in combining internal and external information to achieve organization objectives. It can deepen organization culture, support new staff induction, and remove the inherent security risks involved in important documents being attached to email. Critically, it can capture staff knowledge, so that if they leave, the organization has some record of the expertise they developed.

Unfortunately, there is a strange assumption among some people that purely by placing content on an intranet (no matter how poor in quality), it will automatically become high-quality content that people will want to read. It doesn't work that way.

Like an Internet site, an intranet should be managed by an editor or group of editors who understand the type of content that the organization's staff need. Staff don't somehow "dumb down" when they go to the intranet. If a staff member reads the *Washington Post* over breakfast, they may not expect the same quality of writing when looking at their intranet, but they won't accept the type of poor-quality content that unfortunately often finds its way onto intranets. If staff don't find quality content on the intranet, they will stop using it.

In the early days, senior management often ignored intranets. Little or no standards were applied. It's of fundamental importance now that an intranet strategy is based on organization-wide objectives and standards. Publishing standards are critical to ensure that the right content is published for the right person. Information architecture standards are required so that content is professionally organized and laid out. Remember that an intranet will have far more content than an Internet website. Without a well-thought-out information architecture, the management of content will become a nightmare.

In the modern, often physically dispersed, organization, the intranet might be the one place that every employee can visit every day. In this sense, it can act as a vehicle that communicates organization strategy and culture. Properly designed and run, it becomes the essential glue that helps hold an organization together.

Like all websites, an intranet should focus on what's vital—the content. Keep the pages small as you may have people logging on from outside the office (home, hotels, and so on), and focus on the content that's really important to staff such as essential directories, containing at a minimum phone and email details to facilitate staff communication.

Reasons why intranets fail include the following:

- no clear focus or objectives, resulting in staff losing faith, dismissing the intranet, and going to other sources for their content
- not enough budget, inadequate skills, and lack of training
- poor-quality content and poorly designed information architecture
- staff who are expected to contribute content don't have the time, or the required skills, and they don't see it as part of their job function

IP

Internet Protocol, the protocol that transmits packets of data over the Internet and routes them to their destination.

IP address

This is a computer's unique address on the Internet. They are written as four groups of up to three digits separated by periods, 192.16.45.12. These are translated into domain names (www.cnn.com) by DNS. See also DNS.

IPO

Stands for initial public offering, the first sale of a company's stocks or shares to the general public on the stock market.

Irish punts

See FOREIGN CURRENCIES.

ISDN

Stands for Integrated Services Digital Network, a global communications standard for sending data over digital lines. ISDN lines are often used by businesses because they are faster than standard Internet connections.

ISO

Short for International Organization for Standardization, a non-government, worldwide federation of national standards bodies from 140 countries, one from each country, founded in 1947. ISO is responsible for creating international standards in many areas, including computers and communications. (ISO is not an acronym, or it would be IOS; rather, it comes from the Latin word *isos*, meaning equal.)

See also ABBREVIATIONS AND ACRONYMS.

ISP

Stands for Internet service provider, a company that provides Internet access.

IT

Stands for Information Technology, the use of computer and electronic technologies to process and distribute information.

italics

In italic print or typeface the letters slant to the right. Italics can be hard to read on screen and therefore should be avoided in general text, particularly when used in conjunction with small fonts.

However, certain conventions call for the use of italics. Use italics for

- titles of books, films, plays, long poems, periodicals, including newspapers, magazines, and journals (but don't use italics for website names, even if they are online periodicals)

  The *New York Times* has an excellent style guide.

- works of art, names of ships, foreign words and expressions

  George Elliot was merely her *nom de plume*.

- letters, words, and terms used to refer to the letter, word, or term itself

  An em dash is the width of the letter *m*.

  Kid means goat and *kid* means child.

See also SPECIAL TREATMENT OF WORDS.

its, it's

One of the most common mistakes in the English language. *Its* is the possessive form, *it's* is a contraction of "it is" or "it has":

It's (it is) not easy being this perfect you know.

It's (it has) been a good summer.

The poor animal hurt its paw.

J

Japanese yen

See FOREIGN CURRENCIES.

Java

Java is an object-oriented, secure, platform-independent language created by Sun Microsystems. Currently, its most widespread use is in programming small applications, or applets, for the Web. Its platform-independence makes it very useful because readers access the Web from many different type of computers.

JavaScript

A simple, platform-independent scripting language, developed by Netscape and Sun Microsystems, only loosely related to Java, that adds basic online applications and functions to Webpages. While more limited than Java, it's generally considered easier to write.

job titles

See TITLES (OF JOBS).

JPEG

Stands for Joint Photographic Experts Group and is pronounced "jay-peg." JPEG is the standard compression format for photographs on the Web.

judgment, judgement

Judgment in American English, *judgement* (generally) in British English (*judgment* is reserved for legal works in British English).

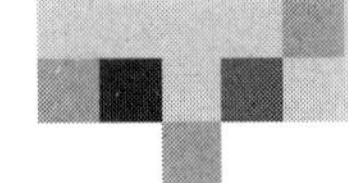

K

K, KB

See KILOBYTE.

keyboard shortcuts

Many people prefer to use keyboard shortcuts where possible, such as "tabbing" between fields in login screens and forms. Not providing keyboard shortcuts adds unnecessary extra steps for your readers and can also cause serious accessibility problems.

keyword

A keyword is a form of metadata. It's a relevant word that describes the content in a document, or that describes a particular website and/or section of a website, to facilitate a reader's search. Keywords are not generally published on the website itself (unless they are included as part of headings) but are embedded in the HTML coding for the website pages using what is called a *metatag*.

Keywords are very important because most people search for content using one or two keywords, rather than a sentence, title, or phrase.

The danger with keywords is that they are often abused. People use too many keywords and/or irrelevant ones in the hope of bringing more people to the document/website. Remember that the function of keywords is to help the reader find the right document/website, and to help the organization find the right reader. Bringing the wrong reader to the wrong document/website serves the purposes of neither the reader nor the organization.

See METATAG, METADATA.

kilobyte

A thousand bytes, abbreviated as K, KB, or (less frequently) Kbyte (note that kilobit is abbreviated as Kb).

knowledge

Knowledge is what we know. From an organizational perspective, knowledge represents the intellectual capacity of its staff to carry out tasks that will create value for the organization. See CONTENT, DATA, INFORMATION.

knowledge capital

Knowledge capital, also known as intellectual capital, expresses the intellectual asset worth, as against the physical asset worth, of an organization. Knowledge capital is more important to the success of a modern organization than physical capital.

Knowledge capital exists in two forms. First, it exists within the minds of the people who have knowledge that will make the organization more productive. Its totality is the collective knowledge of the people who have worked for and presently work for the organization. Second, knowledge capital exists as content. Content is the formal "written-down" expression of knowledge capital. Once knowledge capital has been turned into content it becomes far more useful—and valuable—to the modern organization. A classic example of knowledge capital as content is a patent document.

knowledge management (KM)

Knowledge management is the systematic process of managing what an organization knows to create value. There are two essential aspects of knowledge management that are interdependent. First, you have to get people in person-to-person settings or over networks (email, teleconferencing, videoconferencing) to work better together to create and share knowledge. Then, you need to get people to translate their knowledge into content that can then be shared and used in a much wider setting.

labor, labour

Labor in American English, *labour* in British English.

LAN

Local area network, a network of computers contained in one physical location.

language

The entry on localization touches on websites in other languages. Here the question is which form of English to use—American, British, or even

Australian? Unless the website is aimed specifically at a national or regional audience, use the most inclusive language possible. For an international audience, therefore, it is more prudent to use American English, as most of your readers will be familiar with this. People who use British English are generally familiar with American English and will recognize it as such. Therefore, you will offend fewer people by using American spelling and style conventions. We're not saying that American conventions are right and British conventions wrong (whichever you were taught as a child will seem right), rather we're suggesting a pragmatic approach.

Of course, if your website is designed specifically for people in the British Isles or in nations that were members of the British Commonwealth, you should use British English.

The main differences between American English and British English are

- **Date style:** American English generally places the month before the day so what in British English is 3 August 2001 (3-8-01) in American English is August 3, 2001, (8-3-01). Note the commas surrounding the year. If you include the day of the week, follow it by a comma:

  Thursday, August 3, 2000, was the day he died.

  See DATES.

- **Punctuation:** American English uses the serial comma—place a comma before the "and/or" in a series of three or more items (this is generally not used in British English). American English always places the closing quote after the period or comma (but not after the dash, colon, or semicolon). For example

  "I'm not much of a fan of 'the king,' as she calls him."

  British English, on the other hand, generally places the closing quotation mark after the period or comma only when the quoted matter is a grammatically complete sentence. See COMMA, QUOTATION MARKS.

- **Quotation marks:** American English generally uses double quotes (" "), whereas British English generally uses single quotes (' '). See QUOTATION MARKS.

- **Spelling:** While it might look like a huge task to learn all the differences in spelling, remember that your spell checker will do a lot of the work for you.

This list is not exhaustive, but it does highlight the main differences to watch out for. Remember that not all *ise* endings change to *ize*, etc. Consult a dictionary when in doubt or use your spell checker.

American	British	Example (American)
ize	ise	capitalize
am	amme	gram
ay	ey	gray
ck	que	check, checkered
e	ae	archeology
e	oe	fetal
er	re	fiber
eu	oeu	maneuver
f	ph	sulfur
ing	eing	aging
l	ll	traveler, traveled
ment	ement	judgment
og	ogue	dialog
ol	oul	mold, smolder
or	our	color
ow	ough	plow
sk	sc	skeptical

Other changes	
first, second (in enumerations)	firstly, secondly
forward	forwards
toward	towards
last name	surname

language and geographic navigation

Language tends to be a political and emotive issue. Approach language navigation with sensitivity. Where a website is broken down by country or region, geographic navigation allows the reader to choose a country or region. It may be that in certain circumstances, geographic and language navigation can merge. For example, if you choose Germany, you are also sent to the German language version.

If a website has more than one language, then language navigation needs to be provided. If a substantial majority of the readers use one language, then the homepage can default to this language. You can include the other languages in a separate language-navigation bar on the homepage. On pages other than the homepage, you can provide a drop-down menu. If you have a lot of languages—more than five—you can use a drop-down menu on the homepage rather than the language-navigation bar. If no one language is used by a substantial majority of the readers, a preliminary page needs to be created where the reader is asked to choose their preferred language.

It is not recommended to use a flag icon to signify language, as flags are for nations and don't always appropriately describe the language. For example, Canada has two official languages: French and English. Instead, use the native description for the language. For example, for German use "Deutsche."

See also NAVIGATION.

last updated

This information is normally presented in the footer of a page, informing the reader of when the page was last changed, thus giving an indication of how up to date it is. For example, "Last updated: July 10, 2001." However, this information has lost a lot of credibility because many websites use software code to automatically change the date, regardless of whether the page itself has been changed. Not recommended. See also DATING DOCUMENTS AND SUMMARIES.

laying out a document

See WEBSITE LAYOUT AND DESIGN.

layout and design

See WEBSITE LAYOUT AND DESIGN.

lead

The lead is the opening sentence, paragraph, or paragraphs of an article. The different approaches to introducing a piece of content fall into two categories, direct and indirect. Direct leads are straightforward introductions to the text that follows, such as

> There is a right way and a wrong way to begin a Web article ...

Indirect leads typically begin with quotes or anecdotes. On the Web, simple, direct leads are usually best.

See page 3.

leased line

Permanent private telephone connections leased by businesses from telecommunications companies. Also called a "dedicated line."

less, fewer

See FEWER, LESS.

libel

A false and malicious published statement that damages the reputation of a person or organization. Libel law varies widely from one nation to another. A statement that's clearly permissible in the US, for instance, may be clearly libelous in Great Britain. Within the US, libel law varies widely from state to state. Libel law is highly complex, and is sometimes arcane.

Every publication, online or off, should have an awareness of libel issues and a policy regarding them, and all writers and editors must be familiar with it. Any negative statements about individuals of organizations should be carefully examined to see whether they are potentially libelous, and reviewed by an attorney if there are any questions. It is customary at many publishing companies to have an attorney or paralegal read everything before it's published.

On the Web, the Libel Resource Defense Center (www.ldrc.com/ldrcinfo.html), a non-profit organization of publishers from different media, provides information on libel issues. Offline, *The Associated Press Stylebook and Briefing on Media Law* is a standard reference for journalists in the US, and there are many handbooks and guides dealing with libel issues from national and international perspectives.

See also CORRECTIONS.

line length

Readers have trouble following text that's set in very wide columns. Although the optimal line length will depend on the overall page layout and font size used on your site, in general lines should be narrower than 10 words (about 70 characters). Most print magazines use columns that are shorter still—seven or eight words per line (50 to 65 characters). See also WORD PROCESSORS.

link title

A device that helps the reader know where they will go before they click a link. For example, let's say the following text exists on a page: "Peter James has an extensive bio, having worked and written about the electronics industry for twenty years." With link text, if the reader rolls their mouse over the bio link, they might see extra text such as, "Also allows you to buy books by Peter James."

However, the vast majority of links should be self-descriptive and therefore would not require a link title. Link titles should not be used as a crutch for poorly termed classifications or badly written text.

links

A link (or hyperlink) connects one element in a hypertext document and another element within that document, another file, or script. Links are what make the Web fundamentally different from other media.

A key principle of linking is that the reader should know, if possible, what sections of the website they have already visited and what sections they have not. That is why links change color. All textual links should use the standard industry underline format, blue for unclicked, purple for clicked. Creating different colors for links only confuses the reader. Never underline text that is not a link, as this also confuses the reader. Ideally, text links should be presented on a white background. If, for design reasons, other colors are required, these should be light. Never use dark blue, purple, or black backgrounds.

Never have something linking to itself (circular linking) as that's just wasting readers' time.

Linked text goes to an HTML page. If that is not the case, inform the reader upfront; for example, if the link leads to an audio file. If the link goes to a password protected area, tell the reader. See also LINK TITLES, GETTING LINKED.

Linux

An operating system based on the open-source approach to programming. Linux was invented by Linus Torvalds. In a number of situations, Linux is seen as a viable alternative to the Microsoft operating systems. See also OPEN SOURCE.

lists

In a displayed list, it's a matter of style whether the list stem should have a colon or not. We'd recommend not using a colon unless it's required by grammar.

The colors on the American flag are

1. red
2. white
3. blue

Whether list items begin with a capital and have end punctuation depends largely on the length and content of the items. For example, if the list items are fragments, they should start with a lowercase initial and have no end punctuation. If the list items are full sentences, they should start with a capital letter and have end punctuation. If they are very long, they could start with a capital letter and have no end punctuation (where they are not full sentences). Apply the same format to each item in the same list and the grammatical form of each item in the list should not change.

See also COLONS.

localization

Localization is the process by which a product—or in the case of a website its information architecture and content—is altered so that it is appropriate for another culture or language.

Do not automatically assume that everyone speaks English on the Web. Language can be a very sensitive and political issue (just ask the French or Canadians). It is also predicted that by 2003 almost 70 percent of ecommerce spending will originate outside the US. According to the Aberdeen Group, "if a product or website is not optimized for international transactions, the logistics of marketing to an international market can be crippling, with return rates as high as 46 percent for all products sold internationally."

Localization is not simply a matter of translating text but also of rewriting content, restructuring the classification, and writing new content specifically targeted at your new audience. Professional localization can be an expensive process. Having part of a website in another language is like having a second website, with all the related management and running costs.

When designing a website that is going to be localized, avoid creating graphics and images that have text in them, as this will make the localization process more time-consuming and expensive.

See also LANGUAGE.

log in, login

Log in as verb, login as an adjective (and noun):

> Use your assigned login name to log in to the server.

Similarly with log on (verb) and logon (adjective); log off (verb) and logoff (adjective); and log out (verb) and logout (adjective).

Some writers use these words as a noun, but it is largely frowned upon.

Nonstandard: You will be prompted for your password during login.

logos

A logo is a name, symbol, or trademark designed for easy and definite recognition. Because of bandwidth and screen space constraints, logos should be small. On the Web, you brand with your content rather than your logo. See BRANDING.

All logos should link to the homepage they signify, except when the logo is already on the homepage in question, where it should not be a link. (Never have something linking to itself (circular linking) as it's just wasting readers' time.)

Logos should follow the rules for GRAPHICS.

long documents

See WEBSITE LAYOUT AND DESIGN.

Love Bug

The Love Bug virus damaged companies worldwide when it hit in May 2000. The virus used Microsoft's popular Outlook email program to propagate, and spread rapidly owing to its enticing I LOVE YOU message in the subject field and the fact that recipients were disarmed into thinking that the mail came from somebody they knew. Once the attached program was activated, it quickly replicated itself by automatically sending copies to those listed in the recipient's email address book.

See also VIRUS.

lowercase, use of

See CAPITALIZATION.

Macintosh

Can be abbreviated to "Mac."

magazine names

See ITALICS.

majority

When *majority* refers to a specific number of votes, it takes a singular verb:

> His majority *was* 200 votes.

In general, *majority* refers to "the greater number of a countable set" and is followed by the plural:

> The majority of Americans speak English. (Not "speaks"—they speak individually.)

Don't use it with an uncountable mass, such as work, effort, and so on, or with a single item:

> **Incorrect:** I was doing the majority of the work.
>
> **Incorrect:** The majority of the table was faded.

See also COLLECTIVE NOUNS.

managing editor

This is the person in charge of managing the website. All other functions report to the managing editor. Nomenclature varies among different types of publishing organizations and different companies, with some referring to this position as executive editor or editor-in-chief.

The managing editor is responsible for all major decisions—including, but not limited to, what kinds of content go on the website; how long articles should be in general; how the website is structured; how often content is updated; what the general conventions will be for headlines, fonts, and graphics.

The managing editor function is best performed by a single individual with considerable authority to make decisions and resolve disputes between editors, writers, designers, and information architects. In large and complex organizations, policy may be set by an editorial board, which may also function in a review capacity, but operational authority should be delegated to the managing editor.

See also EDITORIAL BOARD.

masthead

The masthead is the area at the top of a webpage that contains essential descriptive information about the organization (its company name, logo, product name).

There is limited space available on the average computer screen. Remembering that the Web reader is impatient—they come for the content, not the graphics—the masthead area should be kept as small as possible. A masthead should be between 70 and 90 pixels in length, which reflects industry best practice, and allows you to present the maximum amount of content possible to the reader on the first screen.

It should contain the organization's logo, the global navigation, and a search box. The logo and associated graphics should take up no more than 30 percent of the masthead area. If the masthead is dealing with a sub-homepage, it should contain the overall logo of the organization, as well as the title of that particular department, sub-division, product group, and so on. This title should be larger than the company logo to help the reader know where they are on the website. If there is an ecommerce facility on the website, it may contain ecommerce navigation. See Figure 3.9.

FIGURE 3.9

An example layout for a masthead

mcommerce

Ecommerce conducted over wireless or mobile devices.

measurements/symbols

When a number is associated with a unit of measurement, it is normally given as a digit, for example 5 volts, 3 MB. Leave a space between the figure and unit of measurement. However, the money symbol and percent symbol are always closed up. (If an abbreviation (Fr) or currency code (FRF) is used rather than a money symbol, leave a space between it and the figure.)

> 10 MB, 20 Kg, $24, 10%, USD 342 million, Fr 20.

Abbreviated units of measurements have no period and take no *s* in the plural.

> 10 MB, *not* 10 MBs

With abbreviations, capitalization is important, for example *Mb* means *megabits*, but *MB* means *megabytes*.

List of common measurements

Bits per second	bps
Celsius	°C
Centimeters	cm
Dots per inch	dpi
Fahrenheit	°F
Feet	ft
Gigabits	Gb
Gigabytes	GB
Gigahertz	GHz
Grams	g
Hertz	Hz

Hours	hr
Kilobits	Kb
Kilobits per second	Kbps
Kilobytes	KB, K, or Kbyte
Kilobytes per second	KBps
Kilogram	kg
Kilohertz	kHz
Kilometer	km
Liter	l
Megabits	Mb
Megabits per second	Mbps
Megabytes	MB
Megabytes per second	MBps
Megahertz	MHz
Meter	m
Watt	W

megabit

1,048,576 bits (or 1,024 kilobits), abbreviated to Mb, see MEASUREMENTS.

megabyte

1,048,576 bytes (or 1,024 kilobytes), abbreviated to MB, see MEASUREMENTS.

menu, menu options

Follow the interface for capitalization style—if it's capitalized on the interface, then capitalize it in the text:

Select Print Preview from the File menu.

Capitalize the names of elements (such as buttons or toolbars) that do not have a displayed name, for example the Save button might simply be indicated by a graphic of a disk, with no accompanying text. Consult the product's Help file to see what they call the button.

Click the Print button on the Standard toolbar to print your file.

metadata

One word. This is data about data—for example metadata for a document would include the title, summary, and author, as well as classification information and keywords. All Web content should contain appropriate metadata. Otherwise, it will be much more difficult to find.

Metadata helps the reader to find the specific content they want; improves the chances of a particular document being indexed properly by external search engines; allows the reader to refine a search; and ensures that essential legal and/or administrative information is gathered on a particular document (copyright information, and so on).

Unless there is a specific reason not to, every page on the website should have appropriate metadata embedded in its HTML. Otherwise, that page will stand less of a chance of being found and properly indexed by both the internal search engine and external ones.

Metadata must be fundamentally linked to the search process and what readers search by. Only collect the metadata that is truly useful and make sure that all essential information is included. See also KEYWORD.

metatag

One word. Allows for the provision of metadata on a website that does not appear on the website itself. The metatag is embedded into the HTML for any particular page. This metadata is then used by search engines to index the page for future searches. Keywords are the principal form of data entered into metatags, as that is how most people search. See KEYWORD, SEARCH ENGINE REGISTRATION AND OPTIMIZATION.

Microsoft Word

See WORD PROCESSORS.

million

Million is normally spelled out:

10 million (not 10,000,000)

mobile device

Any non-fixed device that can be used to access the Internet, including cellular phones and PDAs.

mobile phones

In the US, mobile phones are referred to as *cell phones*.

modem

A modem is a device that when attached to a computer allows someone to connect to the Internet.

moderator

A moderator is essential to the successful management of online community activities such as discussion boards, chat, and email mailing lists. Moderators are like editors in that they have a quality control function, but they are also a chairperson and evangelist, encouraging contributions and ensuring that everything runs smoothly.

Without quality moderation, online community activities tend to veer toward the chaotic. Everything gets published whether it's good or not and consequently quality contributors leave for moderated environments where their ideas are treated with respect.

A quality moderator should promote and encourage membership; introduce new and interesting topics when required; sift through contributions and publish only the most relevant ones; act as a referee for readers in conflict; and police content from a copyright and libel point of view. See CHAT, DISCUSSION BOARDS, EMAIL MAILING LIST, ONLINE COMMUNITY.

money

Sums of money should be given in figures, irrespective of the amount:

$5, 5 cents, or £10 million, *not* ten million dollars

If a money symbol is used, there is no space between the symbol and the figure. If an abbreviation or currency code is used there *is* a space between it and the figure.

$100 USD 100 Fr 20

Million and billion are generally spelled out.

For a list of foreign currency codes and symbols, see FOREIGN CURRENCIES.

monitor size

See SCREEN SIZE.

months

When a phrase lists only the month and the year, do not place a comma between them. When a phrase lists the day, month, and year, set off the year with commas in American English. See DATES for more information.

May 2001 was a warm month.

July 10, 2001, was their wedding day. (American English)

My start date was 20 June 2001. (British English)

Abbreviate the months as follows (note the periods):

American English:

Jan. Feb. March April May June July Aug. Sept. Oct. Nov. Dec.

British English:

Jan. Feb. Mar. Apr. May June July Aug. Sept. Oct. Nov. Dec.

Moore's Law

In 1965, Gordon Moore, one of the founders of Intel, predicted that computer chips would double in capacity every 12 to 18 months. The pace of change has slowed somewhat and so the definition has been changed slightly to reflect that the doubling occurs every 18 months only. A remarkably accurate prediction nevertheless.

mouse

The plural of mouse is found in a few forms at the moment—*mice*, *mouses*, and even *mouse devices*. We'd recommend using *mice*—it's least awkward and it's the preferred option in the *American Heritage Dictionary*.

mouseclick

One word. See CLICK.

mouseover

One word. Also known as rollovers, mouseovers are created using JavaScript and allow you to change a page element, such as a graphic, when the reader holds the mouse over that element. For example, a link could change color.

mousepad

One word.

MPEG

Stands for Moving Picture Experts Group and is pronounced "em-peg." MPEG is a video and audio compression method on the Web.

MP3

This is the file extension for an MPEG, audio layer 3—a high-quality compressed music file that can be downloaded from the Internet and replayed using PC software or by a special MP3 portable player. See also NAPSTER.

multimedia

Multimedia refers to an environment that uses a combination of media to communicate, such as text, graphics, animations, audio, and video. Multimedia as a term has been more associated with CD-ROMs than with the Internet, due the low bandwidth available online.

During the mid-nineties, multimedia became a hot term for the convergence of media. The multimedia promise has thus far failed to live up to the hype, and the word has lost much of its appeal.

Provide an auditory description of the important information of the visual track of a multimedia presentation for accessibility reasons where possible. See also ACCESSIBLITY.

N

Napster

A web-based peer-to-peer networking system that allows users to access and share songs in an MP3 format. Napster was the subject of much controversy because it enabled people to download commercial music without payment. A number of American court rulings, which threatened to close Napster down, have seen it introduce software to filter out commercial music. Napster has indicated that it will include a payment system.

Nasdaq

Initial capital letter only. The Nasdaq Stock Market is the US stock exchange that specializes in technology companies. (Note that Nasdaq is no longer an acronym.)

navigation

Navigation is the process by which a reader moves through the Web. Strictly speaking there are two basic ways to navigate: by clicking links and by using a search process. However, navigation generally refers to the process of clicking links, with search being treated as a distinct activity. The navigation of a website refers to the set of links the website has. See SEARCH.

If content is the heart of every website publication, then navigation is its brain. When dealing with large quantities of content, the critical importance of quality navigation cannot be overestimated. Content that can't be found can't be read.

Navigation is a website's table of contents. In a traditional publication you have page numbering to help you navigate. You can hold the publication in your hands and flick through it. If it's a large publication, there is usually an index at the back.

You can't hold a website in your hands. You can't get an immediate sense of its size or complexity. You navigate a website one screen at a time. That can prove to be very disorientating it's easy to get confused, to get lost. A reader who gets lost or confused in this attention-deficit economy is likely to hit the Back button. Thus, creating a navigation system that makes the reader feel comfortable and allows them to find the content they want quickly is critical to the success of any website.

Many of the most popular websites (Yahoo, Amazon, eBay) are like directories. Their strength lies in how quickly they can help readers find what they came looking for. It's important to understand that navigation is never the end objective for the reader. It is there to facilitate the reader getting someplace. Navigation works best when the reader hardly knows that it's there. Thus navigation design should always be simple, direct, unadorned, with the overriding objective of helping the reader get to where they want to go.

A trend in Web navigation is to allow the reader to "personalize" the website. Regular readers will have repeated "paths" to specific content areas. Personalization allows them, among other things, to "shorten"

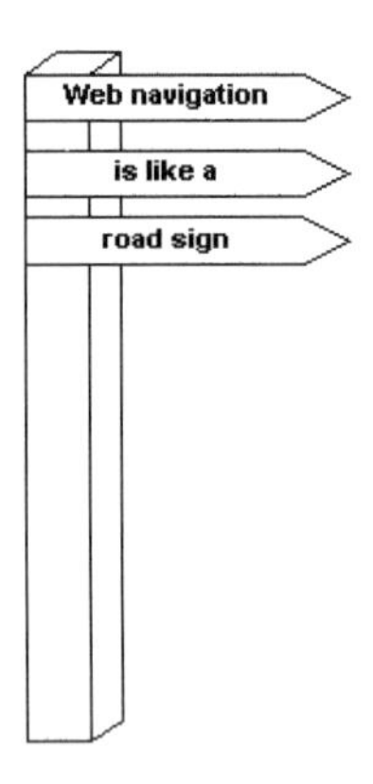

those paths. For example, if they like sport, personalization will allow them to bring their favorite sports links onto the homepage. See PERSONALIZATION.

Navigation and classification are very much intertwined. Where classification is the science of developing a logical order for how content is organized, navigation is the art of presenting the most intuitive and commercial paths through the content for the reader. Navigation is "commercial" in the sense that it will want to point the reader toward areas of the website where the organization can derive most value from the reader visiting. Classification can sometimes be too obscure, but while navigation is more intuitive, it can be too much determined by what you're trying to sell. A balance must be achieved between the two, and keeping the reader's needs as the driving force for both is crucial. While the classification is designed first, it should not be designed in isolation.

Navigation and search are intertwined. Strictly speaking, search is a form of navigation. In many situations, the reader will use a combination of the search function and some navigation options. Remember, most readers are content gatherers. They will use a search to bring them to the subject area or product type they are interested in. Then the navigation should kick in, giving them the context for their search.

Navigation design requires detailed planning. Once launched, it is not something that should be chopped and changed on a whim. You should treat your navigation and classification as if they were written in stone because otherwise you risk confusing your regular readers (customers), something you should avoid at all costs. People are by nature habitual and conservative. If every couple of months you change the structure and navigation of your website, you will risk alienating those who are regular visitors and have got used to your previous navigation and structure.

Outlined here are some of the main navigation design principles:

- **Design for the reader:** The fundamental principle of navigation design is that you should design for the reader and not for purely aesthetic or organizational reasons. To do this successfully, you need reader feedback from day one. Involve the reader by surveying or interviewing them with regard to how they would like to navigate the content. Create mock-ups of the navigation as early as possible and show them to a sample of readers to get feedback.
- **Provide a variety of navigation options:** If everyone wanted to navigate through content in the same way, the job of the navigation designer would be a lot easier. Unfortunately, it's not that simple.

Studies have shown that different readers have different ways they like to navigate around a website. Thus, to facilitate a variety of readers and their navigation requirements, a range of navigation options should be offered.

Navigation options include the following: classification path, core, document, drop-down, ecommerce, global, homepage, language/geographic, personalization, progress chart, related, URL. (See separate listed entries on these options for specific guidelines.)

To deliver a wide variety of navigation options to the reader, an approach of multiple classification of content is required. The Dell website uses multiple classification well. A notebook computer is classified under "Notebooks & Desktops" on the homepage. However, if the reader has clicked on "Home & Office," they will be presented with a link to "Notebooks" on the Home & Office homepage. Notebooks are also classified by country (United States, Germany, Ireland, and so on). This multiple classification allows Dell to provide readers with a wide variety of navigation options. See Figure 3.10.

- **Let the reader know where they are:** Navigation should give the reader a clear and unambiguous indication of what page of the website they are on. Web navigation is like a cross between a map and a system of signposts. Imagine you are on vacation and you are looking at a map in a town square. If the map is well designed, one of the most prominent features will be a "You are here" indicator. CNN supports the reader very well in this regard. For example, if you find yourself on the CNN entertainment page, you will see in bold capitals in the masthead the word "ENTERTAINMENT."

  Although navigation should generally be presented as hypertext, where it is in graphical form the classification name that describes the page the reader is on should be a different design than the other classifications in the navigation. For example, let's say you are on the homepage of a particular website. The "Home" classification in the global navigation should have a slightly different design than the other classifications in that navigation, thus indicating to the reader that they are on that particular page. (This classification should also be unlinked, because otherwise the link will loop to the same page.)

FIGURE 3.10

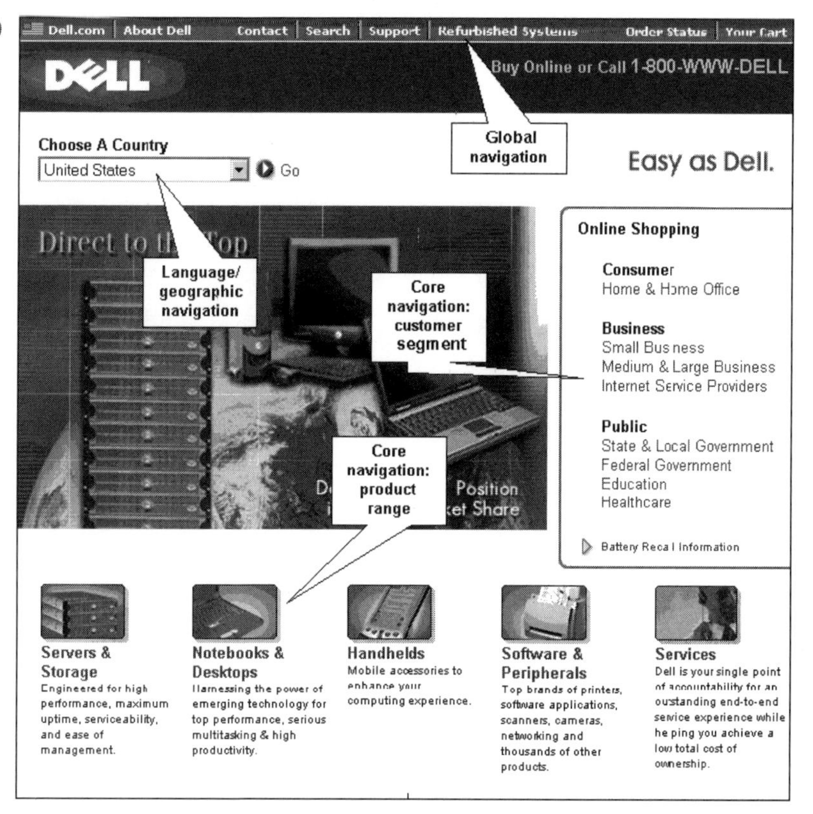

Dell offers a variety of navigation options: global at the top of the page (which includes ecommerce navigation); language/geographic in a drop-down underneath the logo; and two views of the core navigation—product at the bottom, and customer segment on the right.

- **Let the reader know where they've been:** A fundamental principle of Web navigation design is to let the reader know where they've been on the website. That is the key reason for having as much of the navigation as possible in hypertext rather than in graphical form. With hypertext when a link is clicked it changes color. The reader can then know what sections of the website they have visited. This will happen automatically if the navigation is presented as text-based hypertext.

The standard colors for hypertext are blue for unclicked and purple for clicked. Avoid changing these colors. Remember, navigation should always represent the familiar.

- **Let the reader know where they are going:** Navigation should let the reader know where they are going. The obvious way to achieve this is to create navigation classifications that are as self-descriptive as possible. Avoid building navigation based on obscure classifications that are familiar to those who work for the organization but not to the general public, unless, of course, your target readership is organization staff.

  No matter how well the basic navigation is designed, there will be times when it requires extra support to achieve greater clarity for the reader. There are a number of ways to achieve this greater clarity:

  - If the reader clicks a link, they expect to go to an HTML page. If it's a non-HTML page, or a password-protected area, inform them in advance. Tell them they will require a password. Tell them they are linking to an audio file, and so on. Tell them the size of that file. Link to a copy of the software to listen to that file, just in case they don't have a copy.
  - Don't open new browser windows for a reader unless there is a compelling reason. There usually isn't.
  - Change the color of the link when the mouse rolls over it. This is helpful when there are a lot of links close together. Because the link changes color, the reader knows exactly the link they are about to select.
  - Have a drop-down navigation showing lower levels of the classification when the mouse rolls over a particular link. The benefit here is that it allows the reader to jump deeper into the website if they so wish.
  - Where the reader is asked to participate in a process, such as purchasing a product online, progress chart navigation can be helpful. This navigation shows the reader how many stages there are in the process, and where they stand in that process. See PROGRESS CHART NAVIGATION.
  - If the hypertext link is not quite as descriptive as it should be, put in LINK TITLE text to give the reader more background.

- **Provide context:** In a world of 550 billion documents, context is essential. Studies show that in the majority of cases, the reader does not know exactly what content they need. If they do, they will invariably turn to a search process, which offers them the quickest way to get to a particular document.

  Navigation, on the other hand, gives the reader context. It presents content that interconnects. It guides the reader and informs them of content that the organization has that the reader might not have been aware of. This is what context is all about and it's what great navigation does in a seamless, easy-to-follow way.

  For navigation to provide the best possible context, ensure that all content is properly classified, use related navigation that at the end of a document gives links to similar documents, and allow for a variety of product/section homepages that publish the most relevant and positive content for that particular product or section.

- **Be consistent:** Readers particularly turn to navigation when they're confused or lost. Don't confuse them even more by displaying inconsistent or unfamiliar navigation design. For example, if you decide to put the core navigation in the left column, don't then switch it to the right column in another section of the website.

  Consistency of classification is critical for successful navigation. This involves agreeing a content classification that eliminates all duplication and is rigidly adhered to. For example, don't classify a link "Home" in one section of your website and "Homepage" in another section. That only serves to confuse the reader. Establish the classification names at the beginning and use them exactly as you have defined in a consistent manner.

  Consistency of visual navigation design is equally important. Let's say your global navigation is in graphic form, and you've used red buttons with white text for it on the homepage. This design should remain the same throughout the entire website. If you choose blue and purple for your hypertext navigation, don't change these colors in different sections of your website.

  Navigation design requires consistent classification, consistent graphical navigation design, and consistent hypertext color use.

- **Follow Web convention:** Many people instinctively see the Web as a single medium. They like to carry over navigation skills that they acquire on one website to other websites. In this sense, the more similar the navigation of your website is to other websites, the easier it is for the reader to get around your website, based on their experience.

  Over time a number of navigation conventions have emerged on the Web. The designer who deliberately avoids these conventions to be different achieves nothing except confusion for the reader. Confusing the reader is the last thing quality navigation design should do.

  Here's a selection of navigation and classification conventions that have emerged on the Web. It is highly recommended to follow them:

  - Global navigation. This is navigation that runs across the top and bottom of every page, containing links to the major sections of that website. The convention is to begin the global navigation with a "Home" classification. Other commonly used classifications include "About" and "Contact." (See GLOBAL NAVIGATION.)
  - The classification name "Home" is the convention for the name of the overall homepage. Sometimes, in very large websites that have a number of sub-sites, the main homepage is called after the name of the organization, such as Microsoft.com, or zdnet.com.
  - The classification name "About" contains content describing the history, financial performance, business focus, mission statement, etc. of the organization. Sometimes it's used in conjunction with the name of the organization. For example, "About Microsoft."
  - The classification name "Contact" or "Contact Us" contains contact details such as email, telephone, physical address, and map location details.
  - The classification name "Feedback" is used to encourage feedback from the reader.
  - The organization's logo should appear on every page. It should be placed in the top left of the page and should be linked back to the homepage.
  - Where there is core navigation in the body of the page, place it in the left column.
  - The name for the search facility on a website is "Search." The button or link that will initiate the search should be labeled "Search." Search

should also be initiated if the reader presses the Return key. The term for more sophisticated search options is "Advanced search."

- The search box should be available on every page of the website. It should be placed in the top right-hand corner of the page, or near the top left, underneath the logo.
- Every page should have a footer, containing global navigation as hypertext, contact, terms of use, copyright, and privacy links.
- The colors for hypertext are blue for unclicked, purple for clicked.
- If the reader clicks a link they expect that they will be brought to an HTML page. If it's anything else, such as an audio file, inform them in advance.

- **Don't surprise or mislead the reader:** Never bring the reader down a particular navigation path only to lead them to something they do not expect. For example, there are websites where you navigate through a set of links in one language, only to arrive at a document that is in an entirely different language. And it is not uncommon, particularly with American websites, to go through a purchase process to find that the company only ships to the United States. If such a situation is the policy, inform the reader as early as possible in the process in clear, visible, and prominent language.

Navigation design checklist

	Yes	No
Reader designed		
Reader survey		
Reader usability tests		
Navigation options		
Classification path		
Core		
Document		

	Yes	No
Drop-down Ecommerce Global Homepage Language/geographic Personalization Progress chart Related URL		
You are here Prominent page titles Changed navigation colors		
You've been there Blue/purple hyperlinks		
You're going here Non-HTML page identification New browser window identification ALT text Link color change		
Context Proper classification Product/section homepages		

	Yes	No
Consistency Consistent classification Consistent graphical design Consistent hypertext colors		
Familiarity Global navigation on every page Home, About, and Contact links in global navigation Home link first Basic search on every page Basic search top right, or near top left, underneath logo Linked logo on every page Footer on every page		
No surprises No false navigation paths Exceptions prominently highlighted No impossible options		

neither ... nor

When neither and nor link singular terms, use a singular verb. When they link a singular and a plural, use a plural verb.

> Neither Tom nor Harry is here.
>
> Neither Tom nor his brothers are here.

Net

Abbreviation for Internet, no apostrophe, always capped. See INTERNET.

netiquette

Netiquette (from etiquette) is a largely unwritten code for behavior on the Internet. An example of netiquette is keeping your email signature to five lines or less. One of the golden rules of netiquette is not to reply to an email in anger. It's very easy to write a quick response to an email. Always count to 10 before firing off that angry email.

network

A network is an interconnected set of computers. The Internet is a network. The essence of a network is that it allows individuals and organizations to communicate and share information over a common computer-based medium.

new economy

Also known as the information economy, the new economy is fast changing, youthful, digital-based, Internet-driven, networked, information-fueled, and IPO-focused (doesn't have to make a profit). The new economy is looking slightly jaded since the market downturn that began in 2000. However, despite all the hype, there is indeed a new economy emerging that will in time radically alter how the citizens of this world work, play, and learn.

newsgroup

A newsgroup is a pre-Web environment that allows people to discuss issues of interest in an open forum. Newsgroups can be described as an early example of online communities. In the early nineties, newsgroups were very popular, but they became less so as the Web grew. Many newsgroups were replaced by Web-based discussion boards. See also DISCUSSION BOARDS.

newspaper names

See ITALICS.

no one

Two words, singular.

nobody

One word.

non-HTML documents

When readers click a link, they expect to be sent directly to an HTML text page. If instead they are going to initiate the download of an audio, video, PDF, or other non-HTML document, they need to be informed upfront. Also, if they are going to a password-protected area, they need to be alerted.

Clearly inform the reader of the type of document/file (Word, PDF, Excel, RealAudio, etc.) the link will bring them to. State its size. Inform the reader of the software required to run this document/file, and if the software is available online, link to it. If the document is in Microsoft Word or Adobe PDF, provide a sufficient summary in HTML that fully informs the reader of what is in the document. If the reader is being sent to a password-protected area, make a statement such as "Password required."

numbers

Generally, numbers up to and including nine are spelled out, while numbers over nine are given as figures (some organizations choose to spell out numbers up to and including 99):

> I have five bottles of Heineken.

> I have 100 bottles of Heineken.

If a mix of related numbers above and below nine appear in one sentence, use figures:

> Unbelievably, only 2 of the 110 people on the train were injured.

Don't start a sentence with a figure—either rephrase it or spell out the number (even if it's over nine).

The spelling-out-below-10 rule does not apply to ages of people and animals, figures containing decimals, dates and clock time, numbers with percent, units of measurement, sums of money, degrees of temperature, and building numbers.

March 8

a 7-year-old girl

Round numbers can be both digits and words: thousands normally in digits, millions in words. Use commas in four-digit numbers and upward:

1,000

10,000

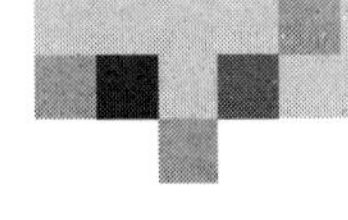

O

object-oriented programming

See OOP.

oblique stroke

See FORWARD SLASH.

offline

One word. *Offline* specifically means not connected to a network, but is also used to refer to the non-web or "real" world.

offline promotion

Remember, a website has no real physical visibility. Without promotion, your potential readers—whether they be staff or customers—may be unaware of your website's existence and what it can do for them.

While it would be wonderful to have a major media campaign promoting your site, for many sites this is just not an affordable option. However, at a minimal cost, you can ensure that your potential audience is at least aware of your site by including the website address prominently on all printed company material. Think constantly of ways to let your potential audience know that your website exists, for example by displaying brochures in your physical place of business (if you have one) promoting the site. If it's an intranet, create posters or leaflets that highlight to employees new or important sections of the website.

See also PROMOTING CONTENT.

on (the) screen, onscreen

Two words as a noun (preferably using *the* or *a*), one word as an adjective:

> The text on the screen is hard to read.
>
> Onscreen text is hard to read.

online

One word. Connected to a network or the Internet.

online community

This is a group of people drawn together on the Internet as a result of common interests. An online community is not framed by where people live. Online communities can be very beneficial from a social point of view, but their commercial benefits are more questionable. However, done right, online communities can be an excellent source of interactivity and content.
See also READER-GENERATED CONTENT.

online reader

People read differently when they're online than when they're reading printed text. The Internet and computer screens still represent relatively awkward technology. It's harder to look at things on a screen than in a magazine. Research by Sun Microsystems (1998) found that reading from computer screens is 25 percent slower than from paper. Online readers tend to be less patient than print readers. On the Web, readers scan pages before they read anything, looking for headings, key phrases, and numbers, and if they're not intrigued by what they see, the Back button is only a mouseclick away. To be a successful Web writer you need to be ever mindful of the itchy finger poised over the mouse.

only (misplaced)

Generally, *only* should be attached to the word or phrase it modifies. Excessive misplacement of *only* can cause ambiguity.

> **Incorrect:** I only swim on Sundays. (I don't eat, sleep, etc.—I only swim.)
>
> **Correct:** I swim only on Sundays.

onscreen capitalization

With onscreen text (on Webpages, interfaces, etc.), as with everything else, the style leans toward lowercase (capitalize the first word and proper nouns only). Lowercase is easier to scan read. See also BUTTONS, CHECKBOXES, MENU, MENU OPTIONS, SCAN READING.

OOP

Stands for object-oriented programming, a type of programming in which programmers can define both the data type that can be applied to a data structure *and* the types of operations (functions) that can be applied to that data structure. The object (data structure) includes both data and functions.

open source

Of or relating to a source code of a software program that is freely available to the public, so that other programers can make additions and improvements. Organizations and individuals do this with the intention of creating a more useful product that is widely available to the Internet community. A basic rule of open source is that any addition or improvement made to the software code must also be made freely available to the community. Examples of open source include the Apache Web server software and the Linux operating system software.

open standards

Open standards relate to a set of rules and approaches to a particular computer environment that are developed and managed by a common, generally non-profit, organization, not controlled by any one organization or group of organizations. The Internet is an example of open standards, and HTML is a specific set of standards evolved for the common use of all. Open standards ensure that the maximum number of individuals and organizations can contribute to and make use of a standard.

opt-in, opt-out

Terms used to describe permission-based newsletters and online services. Subscribers can choose to receive information (opt-in) and can at a later date choose not to receive it any more (opt-out). Double opt-in is becoming the standard. See DOUBLE OPT-IN.

Orwell's rules

The following six rules for writers, defined by the British novelist George Orwell, are the most concise aids to better writing that have ever been written:

1. Never use a metaphor, simile, or other figure of speech that you are used to seeing in print.
2. Never use a long word where a short one will do.
3. If it is possible to cut a word out, always cut it out.
4. Never use the passive [voice] where you can use the active.
5. Never use a foreign phrase, a scientific word, or a jargon word if you can think of an everyday English equivalent.
6. Break any of these rules sooner than say anything outright barbarous.

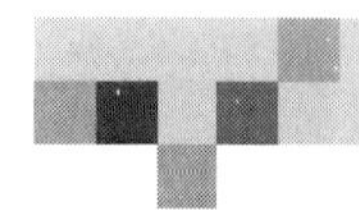

P2P

Peer-to-peer computing. A process where two computers communicate directly without the mediation of a server. One of the best examples of P2P is the Napster service. See NAPSTER.

page

In a Web context, a *page* is normally a Webpage, the entire set of content, navigation, and graphics downloaded to the browser when the reader clicks a link or enters a URL. A page may be made up of a number of screens and may thus require scrolling to move up and down it. Pages should only scroll vertically, not horizontally.

page counter

A small software program that counts the number of visits a Webpage receives and publishes that number on the page. Using a page counter is seen as amateur and is not recommended.

page design

See WEBPAGE DESIGN.

page dimension

See SCREEN SIZE.

page downloads

One of the key ways a reader judges a website is by how quickly its Webpages download. If the pages don't download—appear on the reader's browser—within 10 seconds maximum, the reader is very likely to leave that website. Remember, the overriding characteristic of people who read on the Web is impatience. Some now argue that readers will wait no longer than four seconds.

As first impressions count, homepages in particular should be light, say 40 to 60 KB in file size, with a ceiling of 90 KB for all pages on the site. Page weight is not the only reason for a page to load slowly, but it's certainly the easiest to remedy. You should also consider less straightforward impediments to quick-loading sites such as poor table design, excessive nested tables, and heavy reliance on server-side processing such as CGI scripts. The best way to find out whether your Webpages are downloading quickly is to test the website using average equipment and network speeds.

page impression

A page impression, also known as a page view, is an accepted indicator of traffic to a website that represents a complete Webpage downloaded by a reader. It is a much better indicator of traffic than a hit. See also PAGE VIEW, HIT.

page layout

See WEBSITE LAYOUT AND DESIGN.

page length

Page length is measured by the number of full screens a particular page of content takes up. Optimally, page length should be as short as possible. Under ideal circumstances, a homepage should fit within one screen of an average size monitor and should be no longer than two. Document pages can be longer, but they should not exceed five pages, except under extraordinary circumstances. Of greater importance to the reader is how quickly the page downloads, rather than how long it is. Remember, for the scan reader, the first page counts most. See also PAGE DOWNLOADS, SCAN READING.

page numbers

With very long documents (say 1,500 words or more), you should break up the document into separate pages and provide details on how many pages there are in a "1-2-3-4" linked format at the top and bottom of the page.

Each of the page numbers should be hyperlinked to the appropriate page, except for the page being viewed, which should be unlinked. There should also be a "Previous page" link (on all but the first page) and "Next page" link (on all but the last page). To encourage the reader to click to the next page, it's also a good idea to bring the first subheading from the next page and turn it into a link. (It should link to the top of the next page, and not to the subheading itself.)

FIGURE 3.11

Next page | The way cool generation stakes its claim to China's future
1, 2, 3, 4

An example of a page number approach by Salon.com

See also WEBSITE LAYOUT AND DESIGN.

page size

See PAGE DOWNLOADS.

page title

A page title is a form of metadata. A meaningful page title is important for three reasons. The page title plays an essential role from a search point of view, as the majority of search engines index the page title and display it as the title of the page in the search results, making it the first thing a reader sees. The page title is visible in the Title bar of the browser window. The page title is also used when the page is bookmarked by a reader.

The page title on the homepage should include the critical keywords that indicate what site the reader is entering. For example, the Microsoft homepage has the following page title: "Welcome to Microsoft's Homepage."

On a document page it nearly always makes sense to turn the document heading into the page title, as the heading best describes what is on this page.

Make the page title short, precise, and self-contained (it will be the most prominent aspect of a search result).

page view

Defined as one full page that the reader downloads. Often used to help advertisers get a sense of traffic on a particular page. A page view is the same as a page impression. See also IMPRESSION, PAGE IMPRESSION.

paragraphs

For efficient online reading, paragraphs should be kept shorter than is typical in many kinds of offline writing. As a general rule, average paragraph length on the Web should be no longer than 50 words. For more, see page 8. See also LEAD, WORD PROCESSORS.

parentheses and punctuation

Both the period and the question mark should be placed inside the parentheses only when the parentheses enclose a full sentence. Otherwise, the mark should be outside the parentheses.

> I traveled to London yesterday (and not for the weather).
>
> I traveled to London yesterday. (Needless to say, it was not for the weather.)

Commas, semicolons, colons, and dashes should be dropped before the closing parentheses. Also, in general, they should not come immediately before an opening parenthesis (the exception being numerals or letters in parentheses that mark enumerations in text).

> The site offers clothes (some at half price), books, and glossy magazines.

partner

If your website requires a substantial amount of new content that you cannot create, there may be a real case for exploring partnerships. The ideal partner is one that already has some of the content that you need but is not directly in competition with you.

password

In some circumstances it is necessary to protect content on a website behind a password-based system. All password-protected areas of the website should be clearly flagged with a phrase such as "Password protected."

Allow a subscriber to save the password, to avoid their having to continuously re-enter password details. This can be done with cookie software. (See COOKIE.)

When readers request a password, they should know what they are subscribing to. The best way to do that is to give them an example of the type of content they will get (see SUBSCRIPTION-BASED PUBLISHING). Ask them to first choose a username, offering alternatives if their choice is already in use. Always ask them for their email address as this will be necessary for confirmation. Structure the system so that obviously wrong email addresses will result in an error. In the Password field, ask them to input at least six characters, and advise them to mix text characters with numbers, to make it harder for someone to crack their password. Advise them against using the usual pet's name, etc. Show an "*" for each character entered in the Password field. Ask them to confirm the password.

Where appropriate, allow a successful subscriber immediate access to the website by creating an automatic password verification system. If someone has attempted to reach a password-protected page by clicking a link from another website, for example, send them to that particular page after their subscription has been verified. Email the subscriber a verification and confirmation message, where appropriate.

See CONFIRMATION MESSAGE, VERIFICATION MESSAGE, DOUBLE OPT-IN.

pay-per-view

A model for paying for content on a document-by-document basis. The amount of payment envisaged in most cases would be quite small (cents, pennies). This model has not really caught on because the credit card system is more suited to larger transactions, and an efficient, secure, and widely accepted form of electronic cash has not been developed.

Because quality content is expensive to create and ad revenue alone is generally not a viable business model, some sort of pay-per-view or subscription model is bound to evolve. Otherwise, commercial content has a bleak future on the Internet.

PDA

Stands for personal digital assistant, a handheld device used for basic computing tasks such as keeping personal information, maintaining diaries, sending email, and accessing the Internet.

PDF

Stands for Portable Document Format, a widely used application for electronic document distribution worldwide developed by Adobe Systems. You can create PDFs from a number of Adobe products or you can convert documents from a number of applications into PDF format and retain the fonts, formatting, colors, and graphics of that document. A PDF will display the document to the reader exactly as you intended. It also allows you to prepare a document for printing. PDFs have a relatively light file size. Viewing a PDF requires Adobe Acrobat Reader, which is available free at www.adobe.com and can be run on its own or as a browser plug-in.

Remember that while a PDF allows you to show your document as you want, your aim should be to give the reader what they want, so use PDF only if you think that the reader would like the document in that format (for example if they are likely to want a print copy), or if it is simply not economic to prepare the document in a Web format.

PDFs are anathema to scan readers, and are not picked up by most search engines. So, if you are publishing a PDF on the Web, make sure you have an HTML-based heading and summary associated with it.

See also ACCESSIBILITY.

percent, per cent (%)

Spell it out in text rather than using the symbol %. One word (usually) in American English, two words in British English. Use figures (rather than words) with *percent* (except when it starts a sentence):

10 percent

Usage: *Percent* can take a singular or a plural verb depending on what is being described. Generally, what determines the form of the verb is the noun nearest to it.

> Over 90 percent of people are literate. ("people" plural)
>
> Less than 10 percent of this group agrees. ("this group" singular)

When writing *percent* in an email, use the word rather than the symbol, as symbols are not well translated by many email software programs.

See also COLLECTIVE NOUNS.

period

Period in American English, *full stop* in British English. In American English, periods are always inside quotation marks. Only one space should be given between sentences. See also PARENTHESES AND PUNCTUATION, QUOTATION MARKS.

personal digital assistant

See PDA.

personalization

The use of technology to serve up a unique version of a Webpage according to a reader's behavior and/or preferences. A key benefit of personalization for the regular reader is that they can create navigation shortcuts that allow them to get to the content they want faster. An excellent example of personalization is where Amazon.com recommends books to its customers based on the type of books they have previously purchased.

Personalization is a complex and expensive process that really requires a very large quantity of content and a substantial number of readers before it makes sense. Personalization is no magic answer. Poor-quality content that is personalized is still poor-quality content. However, studies show that regular readers prefer a personalization option.

Personalization has privacy implications because you need to collect information on the reader's habits and preferences if you are to personalize for them. Readers should be kept fully informed of what information is being collected on them. See PRIVACY.

petabytes

1,125,899,906,842,624 bytes (1,024 terabytes), abbreviated PB.

phone, fax numbers

Generally, phone numbers are referred to in the form

Tel: +353 1 818 1000

Tel: +1 212 358 1775

Fax: +353 1 883 0379

The "+" means that the caller dials their own international dial code first, for example to dial an international number from Ireland, you first dial 00. Spaces between the different parts of the number are preferable to punctuation as different countries punctuate them differently.

pixel

Short for picture element, the dots that make up an image on a computer or TV screen, and on paper by a printer. The more pixels, the better.

plagiarism

To use and represent the writings of another person or organization as one's own. The ability to "cut and paste" content makes plagiarism seductively easy on the Web, and it is emerging as an area of serious concern. Every publishing organization needs to have policies and procedures in place regarding plagiarism. There are two different levels of concern:

- **Intentional plagiarism:** Policy here should be unambiguous—plagiarism is unethical, and in some cases illegal. In knowledge-based organizations and in the information economy in general, few types of misconduct are more worrisome. Managers of a website must make sure that all editors, writers, and other members of the publishing team understand this. Any offenses should be treated seriously, at the least by formal reprimand, and possibly by termination of employment. Any accusations of plagiarism by readers should be reviewed at the most senior levels, and a formal policy should be in place for dealing with them. Don't assume that "it can't happen here." There have been many notorious instances of intentional plagiarism at some of the world's most highly regarded publishing organizations.

- **Unintentional plagiarism:** In researching, writing, and editing content, it is all too easy to incorporate someone else's writing inadvertently. There's nothing wrong with using the ideas and opinions of others in an article or other written work—writers must simply make sure that the sources of opinions and ideas are noted and attributed correctly, and that they have not merely cut and pasted someone else's writing into their own. The best way to avoid unintentional plagiarism is to insist on a rigorous and formal fact-checking process.

See also FACT CHECKING, ATTRIBUTION, REFERENCING ONLINE SOURCES.

plain text

Text containing no formatting or special coding. See also ASCII.

platform independent

Platform-independent entities are either not dependent on any particular computer operating system (Windows, UNIX), or can be easily ported from one computer operating system to another. Java was developed as a platform-independent programming language. The Internet is a platform-independent environment.

plug-in

Hyphenated as both noun and adjective—a tool that "plugs" into a Web browser to provide added functionality.

political terms

Capitalize the term, and the word *party*, when referencing a particular party, lowercase when referring to a philosophy (left, right, communist, etc.):

> He is a former Republican (a member of the Republican Party).
>
> She confessed she had communist leanings.

portal

A website that acts as the reader's gateway to the Internet. Portals offer a broad array of services including search engines, directories, email, chat rooms, and bulletin boards. See also VORTAL.

possessives

The possessive case of a singular noun is formed by adding *'s*. Although some people simply add an apostrophe to singular nouns ending in *s*, the *'s* better reflects how it is actually pronounced:

> Charles's *not* Charles'

Exceptions to this are "Jesus" and "Moses," where you add the apostrophe only.

prepositions to watch

> accountable *to* or *for*
>
> accuse *of*
>
> acquit *of*
>
> affiliate *with* or *to*

agree *on* (a point), *with* (a person or opinion)

ally *to* or *with*

aloof *from*

analogy *between* or *with*

angry *with*, not *at*

annoyed *by, at,* or *with*

aspire *to*, *after,* or *toward*

bored *with* not *of*

charge *with*

comprise (no preposition, see COMPRISE)

consider (no preposition, don't use *as*)

contrast *to* (something opposite), *with* (something different)

convict *of*, not *for*

convince *of*, *that*, not *to* (but can persuade *of*, *that*, and *to*)

compare *to* (when likening), *with* (to contrast)

correspond *with* (a person), *to* (a thing)

decision *made* (in American English), *taken* (in British English)

die *of* (not *from*)

differ *from* (not *to* or *than*), *with* (a person when disagreeing)

different *from* or *than* (not *to*). See DIFFERENT FROM/THAN

fed up *with* (not *of*)

glad *at* (some news), *of* (a possession)

impatient *for* (a thing), *with* (a person)

jealous *of*

part *from* (a person), *with* (a thing)

preferable *to*, not *than*

protest *at*, *against*

reconcile *to* (a thing), *with* (a person)

superior *to*, not *than*

taste *of* (food), *for* (culture, etc.)

Avoid compound prepositions such as *in regard to, in connection with*.

printing

Reading is difficult on the Web and many readers will want to print out documents to read offline. Ideally, a "printer-friendly version" of every document should be provided.

The print version should contain the entire document (but without any irrelevant graphics), the publication date, author name, organization name and contact details, copyright information, and the URL for the Web version of the document.

If printer-friendly versions cannot be supplied, ensure you use the three-column approach to document page layout, with the body of the document in the center column, which ensures that part of the document will not be cut off when printed out.

See also WEBSITE LAYOUT AND DESIGN.

privacy

Privacy is one of the most critical issues that content publishers face on the Internet. Because of a lack of clear legislation, Internet privacy has often been abused. People are thus wary of giving away personal information. They are increasingly concerned about websites that collect information on them without their knowledge, and take a very negative view of websites that they feel are in any way abusing their privacy.

Reader privacy is a particularly important issue when it comes to establishing a subscription-based publication service, or where a personalization system is being implemented. There are three basic principles that need to be employed when you are collecting personal information on a reader:

- inform the reader of what information you wish to collect;
- clearly articulate the uses this information will be put to and the benefits that will accrue to the reader;
- allow the reader the right to view and delete information that has been collected on them.

privacy policy

The page footer should include a link to the privacy policy, which can be on a page of its own or a section in the Terms of use statement. The privacy policy should include information on whether the organization releases information to third parties; what it does with information submitted to the site and how the visitor can control it; and what it does with automatically collected info (type of browser, etc.), cookies, and so on. See also FOOTER, TERMS OF USE STATEMENT.

progress chart navigation

Progress chart navigation is highly recommended where the reader is expected to complete any process that involves more than two steps, for example, purchasing a product online or filling out a long form. Progress chart navigation clearly shows to the reader in linear chart form the number of steps involved in a process, and the steps that the reader has already completed. It should be displayed prominently near the top of the page.

Remember, readers are impatient. If they cannot get an immediate sense of the length of the process, they are likely to hit the Back button. It is also true that many readers are hesitant and unsure when using the Web. Presenting them with a clear progress chart can make them more comfortable.

FIGURE 3.12

1 SHOPPING CART 2 ACCOUNT 3 SHIPPING 4 PAYMENT 5 VERIFY 6 CONFIRM

An example of progress chart navigation from the Iomega website. The filling line, underneath the six stages, shows that the prospective purchaser has completed three out of the six stages in the purchase process.

See also NAVIGATION.

promoting content

Information overload is one of the most critical problems facing the information society. If your reader can't find your content, or doesn't know it exists, they're not going to be able to read it. Promoting content involves bringing the reader to the website and highlighting specific documents or areas for that reader.

There are many different ways to promote content that don't involve spending big budgets on TV or press advertising.

- **Homepage promotion:** A central function of the homepage is to promote key content within the website. Larger websites will have numerous second-level homepages. These homepages should promote key content within their particular section.
- **Internal banner advertising:** A banner advertising system is a useful tool to promote important content. To have a faster download and thus better first impression for the reader, many websites avoid having banner ads on the homepage, or have a smaller banner ad on homepages. See BANNER AD.
- **Email marketing:** Email newsletters are a good way of encouraging the reader to re-visit the website. You can also place advertising text in the newsletter, but remember to clearly differentiate it from editorial content. See EMAIL MARKETING, EMAIL NEWSLETTER.
- **Email signatures:** Email signatures are a good way to promote the content on your website. Employees send a lot of emails every day and if a short promotion is put in each signature, it can deliver a lot of exposure. See EMAIL SIGNATURE.
- **Breaking news:** Breaking news deals with essential content that needs to be promoted immediately and as widely as possible throughout the website. See BREAKING NEWS.
- **Search engine registration and optimization:** Search engines are one of the primary ways that visitors will find your website. Search engine optimization ensures that your Webpages are accessible to search engines and focused in ways that help improve the chances they will be found. See SEARCH ENGINE REGISTRATION AND OPTIMIZATION.

- **Getting linked:** When other websites link to yours it's like embedded word of mouth and is a powerful means of promoting content. Alexa.com gives information on how many links a website has. See GETTING LINKED.
- **Offline promotion:** You don't have to spend a fortune on media campaigns, but you do need to think of ways to make your potential readers aware of your site by, for example, putting up posters in the lunchroom if you're promoting an intranet. See OFFLINE PROMOTION.

publication (noun)

A book, magazine, document, or website that contains content that is available to a readership. Think of your website as a publication and the objectives of your website become clearer. Your website is a publication containing content and other resources that are useful to your target readers.

publication schedule

The publication schedule defines how often new content will be published on a website. A publication without a publication schedule is unprofessional.

Key questions need to be addressed when developing a publication schedule, such as how many new documents a day/week are to be published? How often should the homepage be updated, or how often should email newsletters be published? You need to balance how frequently the reader would like to see new content with the cost of doing so. The more frequent the publication schedule, the more expensive the process. Once a publication schedule has been established, it must be rigidly adhered to. If the homepage is to be "published" at 9 A.M. every weekday, then it must be published at 9 A.M. on the dot every weekday.

publishing

Publishing is the process of creating and distributing content. To be commercially successful, publishing must get the right content to the right person at the right time and at the right price. What differentiates the practice of publishing from data or content management is that publishing takes only the *best* content and publishes it to a targeted readership.

Therefore, publishing alleviates information overload by publishing only the content the readers need. Data and content management often exacerbate information overload by putting in front of the reader vast quantities of content, some of it relevant, some of it not. See also CONTENT MANAGEMENT, DATA MANAGEMENT, INFORMATION OVERLOAD.

pull quotes

A small text passage that is enlarged and set apart from the main text. Because people scan read on the Web, pull quotes can be very helpful in getting them to read on. Pull quotes should be short, no more than 10 to 15 words. They may be placed within the body of the document, or in the left or right column.

From a presentation point of view, the key issue is emphasis. They should stand out in size and in format (bold or a different color can be useful). Another method is to place them in their own box, with the box having a slightly different color background. Don't overuse this facility—once every five to six paragraphs is sufficient.

pull technology

Also known as "pull medium," pull technology publishes content in a Web environment for a reader to visit and read. The primary example of pull technology is the Web browser. The principle here is that quality content "pulls" the reader to the website.

With pull technology the reader is very much in control, deciding exactly when and what content they want to see. However, the reader must also actively decide every single time to go to the website in question. With millions of websites out there it is becoming an increasing challenge to attract readers and keep them coming back. Therefore, most websites also seek to use "push" technology, such as email. See also PUSH TECHNOLOGY.

pure-play

Pure-play is a stock-trading term that refers to ownership in a company that focuses in one area to the exclusion of other markets. Increasingly, pure-play is also used to refer to an organization that trades only on the Internet, and has no physical outlets. See also DOTCOM.

Pure-play was initially seen as a cost-effective business model in that there were no physical store costs. However, pure-plays lacked visibility in front of the consumer and therefore had to spend extensively on marketing.

A great number of pure-plays have gone out of business because of low brand awareness, high marketing costs, and, increasingly, competition from established offline brands with clicks-and-mortar strategies. See also CLICKS AND MORTAR.

push technology

Also known as "push medium," push technology sends content directly to a reader either by email, browser plug-in, or some other piece of software. In essence, push technology is an example of subscription-based publishing. The classic example of push technology is an email newsletter.

Properly used, a push approach makes a lot of sense. Instead of a reader having to decide every time to go to a website (pull technology), they can sign up for an email newsletter or other push media and get content sent to them on a regular basis.

However, push technology has suffered from improper use and extreme hype. Some organizations pushed too much content, which overwhelmed readers and upset network administrators, who saw their network slow to a crawl. A push approach works well if a limited quantity of very specific content is sent to a highly targeted readership.

Often the best approach is a combination of the push and pull technology. For example, an email newsletter (push) is distributed containing short content summaries, with links back to the website (pull) for the full document. See EMAIL NEWSLETTER, PULL TECHNOLOGY, SUBSCRIPTION-BASED PUBLISHING.

Q

question marks

Question marks denote direct queries. Indirect questions do not require a question mark.

He wondered whether he should go home.

quotation marks

Quoted matter, spoken or written, is enclosed in double quotation marks in American English. Single quotation marks are used for quotations within quotations. British style is normally the reverse (single outer, double inner).

Use a comma before a direct quotation of only a few words following an introductory phrase:

> Then she said, "If she thinks I'm going to say 'I don't mind, go ahead,' she can think again."

Closing punctuation: American English follows what is known as the conventional order of punctuation. Periods and commas are always inside the closing quotation mark; dashes, semicolons, and colons are always outside the quotation mark; and exclamation points can go either way depending on whether the exclamation point is for the whole sentence or just a portion of the sentence.

> "This man," he said "is not my father." (American English)
>
> Then she said, "You'll come to a bad end someday!" (American English)

British English generally follows what is called the logical order of punctuation, where the closing quotation mark comes after the period or comma only when it contains a grammatically complete sentence (has a subject and verb, usually starting with a capital letter).

> I replied, "I hated her." (British English)

In continuous quoted material that is more than one paragraph long, place opening quotation marks at the beginning of each of the paragraphs, but place closing quotes at the end of the last paragraph only.

quotations

Because text in italics is not easy to read on screen, it is better to avoid having long sections of italicized text. Therefore, as quotations can be quite long, don't put them in italics.

Quotations are sacrosanct—they should reproduce exactly the wording, spelling, capitalization, and internal punctuation of the original, except that single quotation marks may be changed to double, and double to single as house style prescribes, and commas or periods outside the closing quotation mark may be moved inside. A few other changes are allowed to make the passage fit smoothly into the work in which it is quoted, including changing the initial letter to a capital or lowercase letter, omitting the final period or changing it to a comma as required, and omitting punctuation where ellipsis points are used, correcting obvious typographical errors in modern works (preserve idiosyncrasy of spelling in older works).

Quotations may be incorporated in two ways: run in (integrated in the text and enclosed in quotation marks) or set off from the text, without quotation marks (often called "extracts," normally used for long quotations). Be aware of verb agreement when incorporating parts of a quote. If a quote is difficult to incorporate as is, the best solution might be to change it from a direct to an indirect quote. You can omit parts of a quote but you should always indicate this by inserting an ellipsis (…) where the missing material would be.

> "To be or not to be … is the question."

If a change in the original is required to help the reader understand, place the text you have added or changed in square brackets.

> "He [Coleridge] talked on for ever; and you wished him to talk on for ever."

See also ELLIPSIS, QUOTATION MARKS.

R

RAM

Stands for random-access memory, the computer's short-term memory.

reader

A reader is a person who reads content. *The Web Content Style Guide* defines the person who visits a website as a reader, rather than the more generic term "user," because the primary thing a person does on a website is read. Thinking of a website as a publication and the people who use the website as readers helps you focus on the essentials: basically, if nobody reads your website, it's a failure, no matter how technically sophisticated it may be.

reader-generated content

A key difference between Internet publishing and traditional publishing is the reader interaction possible on the Internet.

Reader-generated content is facilitated by mailing lists, discussion boards, chat, customer review boards, and so on. Properly done, reader-generated content encourages reader participation and feedback, creates cost-effective content for the website, and builds a sense of community that will generate repeat visits and a sense of loyalty. It will help you figure out what your customers want.

Reader-generated content tends to be most effective in community-oriented or entertainment-oriented websites, or in websites where you want to encourage the free flow of ideas and interaction.

It is very important to establish clear policies and procedures with regard to how such content will be managed. In particular, a clear policy statement needs to be made available to all readers who wish to contribute content. It should cover copyright with regard to the content contributed, all libel and legal issues, and termination conditions.

reader identification

You need to identify your reader before deciding what content to present them with. Depending on the nature of your publication, there can be different levels of defining your reader. For example, some websites are targeted at individuals living in a specific geographic area (say, an ISP that has access numbers for only a small area), while others are targeted at very technical readers who are extremely knowledgeable about a particular subject, and who may come from anywhere in the world. Others, such as many intranets, are targeted at busy sales reps on the road.

See also CONTENT ACQUISITION.

reader interaction

See INTERACTIVE.

reader, understanding the

See ONLINE READER.

referencing online sources

How scholarly your site is will determine how much you will use citations, references, and bibliographies. For a detailed outline of how to cite and refer to online sources, see *The Columbia Guide to Online Style*.

However, whenever you quote from or use information from another website, it is good practice to provide a proper reference. To avoid long interruptions in the body of the text, you could provide a References list at the bottom of the page. This should contain as much of the following as possible:

- author's name (last name first)
- document title
- website title
- date of Internet publication
- date you accessed it
- <URL>

related navigation

This is navigation that occurs at the end of a document. It gives a selection of documents that have been classified under the same classification as that document, and/or Webpages that relate to the document in question (see Figure 3.13).

FIGURE 3.13

RELATED STORIES:

U.S. Coast Guard picks up 19 Cubans off Florida
September 18, 2000
Qatar Airways jet hijacked; man gives himself up
September 14, 2000
Jordan reportedly foils bid to hijack flight to Damascus
July 5, 2000
Jilted husband parachutes from Philippine plane after hijacking
May 25, 2000

RELATED SITES:

Opa-Locka Airport
Ft. Lauderdale Hollywood International Airport
Federal Aviation Administration
United States Coast Guard Florida Air National Guard
Jane's Online
Jane's Catalogue: Jane's All The World's Aircraft
Boschaero AN-2 Antonov Colt
Aviation Images, Antonov An-2 Colt

An example of related navigation as used by CNN

Related documents should be presented first. They should be ordered by date, the most recent first. The text for the links should be the heading of the documents, which should be hyperlinked to those documents. Related Webpages should follow the same rules as for related documents.

There should be a clear break between the end of the document and the related navigation, perhaps with a line of text such as "Related documents/websites."

See also NAVIGATION, REFERENCING ONLINE SOURCES.

reports

When citing a report, always tell your readers how to access the report for themselves. See also REFERENCING ONLINE SOURCES.

reusing content

See CONTENT ACQUISITION.

rollover

See MOUSEOVER.

ROM

Stands for read-only memory, a storage device that stores read-only content (content that can't be altered).

router

A router is a device connected to at least two networks that decides the next network path to send a data packet, based on its communication with other routers.

S

sans serif

See FONTS.

scan reading

Scan reading involves skimming across navigation and content, picking out headings, summaries, the first sentences of paragraphs, and so on. Studies from the Stanford Poynter Institute and Useit.com have found that scan reading is emerging as the dominant form of reading on the Web.

To meet the needs of scan readers, navigation needs to be clear and consistent; content needs to make effective use of headings, subheadings, pull quotes, and short, snappy summaries; paragraphs and documents need to be short; and hypertext should be used appropriately.

Scan readers (and therefore Web readers) dislike poorly designed navigation, badly laid-out content, vague headings and summaries (or none at all), slow-downloading pages, and content that requires them to download some kind of plug-in.

scannability

The scannability of a particular Webpage relates to its ability to be scan read in the most efficient manner. See SCAN READING.

screen magnifier

A software program that magnifies a portion of the screen so that it can be viewed more easily. Screen magnifiers are used primarily by individuals with poor vision.

screen of content

A screen of content is as much of the content as the reader sees in their browser without having to scroll. See PAGE LENGTH, SCROLL.

screen reader

A software program that reads the contents of the screen aloud. Screen readers are used primarily by the blind. Screen readers can usually only read text that is printed, not painted, to the screen.

screen size

Also known as monitor size. The traditional dimension for Webpages was 640 pixels wide × 480 pixels long, as this reflected the average screen size of monitor available to readers. However, over the past couple of years, the greater majority of readers have computers with monitors that can accommodate a page dimension of 800 pixels wide × 600 pixels long. It is therefore recommended to use the 800 × 600 dimension as this gives much greater scope from a layout point of view. (The design width should actually be 760 pixels, to allow for the scroll bar on the right.) However, if you know that a particular set of target readers have smaller sized monitors, you may have to use a 640 × 480 dimension.

scroll

Scrolling on a Webpage should only move the page up or down—never ask a reader to scroll horizontally. Some thinking, borrowed from CD-ROM design, dictated that the reader should not have to scroll at all—that all content should be presented on a screen-by-screen basis. This does not work on the Web as clicking to the next screen is generally more time-consuming, due to bandwidth constraints. Thus, readers prefer to scroll.

When designing a Webpage, keep in mind that a page that requires a lot of scrolling will generally be larger in file size, and if it takes too long to download, the primary time-saving benefit of scrolling versus clicking is lost. Homepages and sub-homepages should generally be no more than two screens. Scrolling works best in document pages where it is obvious to the reader that they need to scroll down to read more of the content. Generally, the deeper a reader gets into a website, the more they are willing to scroll.

search

In a search process, the reader enters a keyword or term into a search box, and a search engine then returns relevant content that matches. There are two broad types of search: basic and advanced.

When establishing a search facility on your site, follow these conventions. The search should begin with the touch of the Return key, as well as the click of the Search button. The ideal font for the search box is Arial, as Arial is a narrow font and allows the reader to enter more characters. The basic search box should appear on every page on the website, preferably in the top right, in the masthead, or near the top left, just underneath the organization logo.

- **Basic search:** All but the smallest of websites should offer at least a basic search facility. Basic search should be accessible from and clearly visible on every page on the site. The MASTHEAD is a good place to position it.

  Basic search should include an edit box sufficiently large to enter 15 to 20 characters, a button to the right of the edit box labeled "Search," a text link underneath the edit box labeled "Advanced search" (if you have one).

  The initial target of the basic search should be the contents of the entire website. The basic search should allow for Boolean commands (AND, OR, etc.), although this does not need to be explained.
- **Advanced search:** An advanced search allows the reader to do more complex searches. The more comprehensive the CLASSIFICATION system and the METADATA collected, the more options you can provide in an advanced search. See Figure 3.14.

  The edit box should allow longer entries (between 30 and 50 characters) than the basic search. A "Help" link, close to the Search button, should be provided on how to use the advanced search functionality. The advanced search should, of course, allow for Boolean commands.

  The advanced search screen should display the appropriate metadata and classification collected on the content. For example, if the content was classified by country, product type, date, author, etc., the reader should be able to refine their search using these classifications.
- **Boolean search:** A Boolean search allows you to directly connect two or more words in a search process. The key Boolean commands are "AND," "OR," and "NOT." Boolean is generally an advanced search feature, although most basic search boxes will take Boolean commands.

  Boolean search is not well understood by most people, and should always be supported by comprehensive help. To simplify Boolean search, options such as "with all the words," "with the exact phrase," "with any of the words," and "without the words" should be available. See also SEARCHING TIPS.

FIGURE 3.14

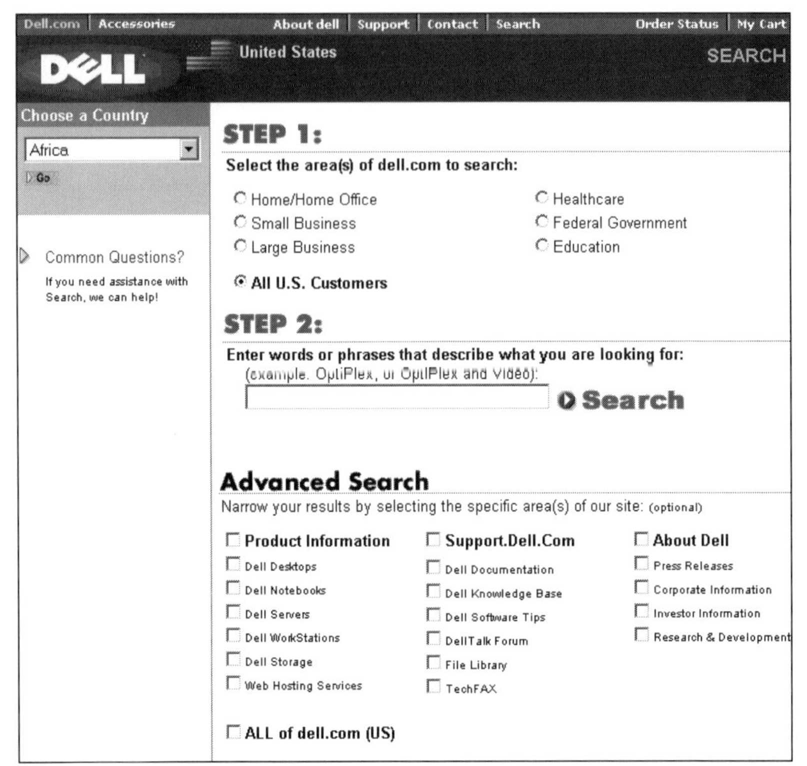

An example of advanced search from Dell

- **Laying out search results:** Search results should show results in the order of relevance. They should not show duplicate entries of content. This includes multiple URLs pointing to the same piece of content. Each search result should show the title of the document, hyperlinked, a two-line summary of the document, and the searched-for word or phrase highlighted in the result.

  Show the size of the page that is being presented (29 KB). The URL for the document should be displayed unlinked, on a separate line. Show the date the document was published. A "more like this" facility, linking to the classification that the specified search result was classified under, can be useful.

The number of documents found should be displayed between the top search box and the actual results. The basic search box should be displayed at the top of the search results and at the bottom. The search keyword(s) used in the search process should also be displayed in the box.

If the reader has been searching using basic search and then decides to use advanced search, bring any search keywords that the reader has input into the basic search box and place them in the corresponding advanced search box.

In the case of an advanced search, present the basic search box at the top of the search results and at the bottom.

The search results should be broken down into batches of 10. At the end of each batch of results should be a set of links to the other batches up to the 10th batch (for example, 1 2 3 4 5 6 7 8 9). "Next" and "Previous" links should be provided. "Next" links you to the next page, "Previous" to the page before.

The document the reader selects from the search results should show the reader's query text highlighted within the document, allowing the reader to determine the relevance of that document to their query. See Figure 3.15.

search directory

A search directory depends on editors to select the best websites in appropriate classifications and present them to the reader. Yahoo is an example of a search directory. Basically, a search directory takes a publishing approach, whereas a search engine takes a purely technological approach. With a search directory, editors decide the classification approach and the most important websites that should go under each classification. A search directory gives the reader limited choice, as against a vast choice from a search engine. The success of Yahoo shows that the average reader prefers to be given a limited choice of the best results. See SEARCH ENGINE.

FIGURE 3.15

Advanced Search   Preferences   Search Tips

metadata   Google Search

Searched the web for **metadata**.

Category: Reference > Libraries > ... > Technical Services > Cataloguing > Metadata

Metadata at W3C
... Metadata and Resource Description. **Metadata** is machine understandable information for the web. The **...**
Description: **Metadata** research at the World Wide Web Consortium.
Category: Reference > Libraries > ... > Technical Services > Cataloguing > Metadata
www.w3.org/Metadata/ 3k Cached Similar pages

Dublin Core **Metadata** Initiative (DCMI)
... The Dublin Core **Metadata** Initiative is an open forum engaged in the development of interoperable online **metadata** standards that support a broad range of **...**
Description: Official page of the Dublin Core **Metadata** Initiative.
Category: Reference > Libraries > ... > Cataloguing > Metadata > Dublin Core
dublincore.org/ - 21k - Cached - Similar pages

Digital Libraries: **Metadata** Resources
... Metadata is data about data. The term refers to any data used to aid the identification, description and location of networked electronic resources. Many **...**
Description: IFLA collection of Internet **metadata** resources.
Category: Reference > Libraries > ... > Technical Services > Cataloguing > Metadata
www.ifla.org/II/metadata.htm - 101k - Cached - Similar pages

UKOLN **Metadata**
Metadata. UKOLN. Projects. We are participants in the following projects which relate to resource description: **...** Initiatives. **...** Registries. **...** What is **metadata**? **...**
Description: Resources from the UK Office for Library and Information Networking
Category: Reference > Libraries > ... > Technical Services > Cataloguing > Metadata
www.ukoln.ac.uk/metadata/ - 6k - Cached - Similar pages

An example of a search results page from Google

search engine

A search engine is a program that searches for keywords in files and documents found on the Web. Popular search engines include Google and AltaVista. (Yahoo is a search directory.) Most websites have a search engine that trawls the contents of that website.

The way a search engine works is that it sends out a piece of software, called a spider, to index the pages on a website, which it then compiles. When a reader searches a search engine they are not actually searching the Web but rather an index of the Web. That is why search results can be delivered so quickly.

A key problem with search engines is that the Web has become so vast that it is becoming impossible to index it all. Studies have indicated that even the most comprehensive search engines are indexing less than 20 percent of Webpages. Also, because of the indexing approach, search engines are not good for finding content that has recently been published.

search engine registration and optimization

Search engines are one of the primary ways that readers find websites. That's why a website with a good search engine listing may see a significant increase in traffic. An excellent website for information on optimizing your listing in search engines is Search Engine Watch (www.searchenginewatch.com).

- **Know how search engines work:** Everyone wants a good listing, but unless you consider how search engines work, you could receive a poor ranking. Making your webpages accessible to search engines and maintaining them in a way that improves their chances of being found can help you. This is search engine optimization.
- **Use keywords:** Use keywords that people are likely to search by to get to your content. Place them in the important locations on the page, such as the page title, but ensure that these keywords reflect what is on the page itself.
- **Use HTML links:** Image maps and frames can cause problems for some search engines, so anticipate that. Avoid using images for navigation links as the search engine might not be able to follow the image maps and won't get past your homepage. Use HTML links instead (using footers also helps). Some search engines cannot follow frame links, so make sure there is another method for them to enter the site, for example through metatags. See FOOTER, GLOBAL NAVIGATION, METATAGS.

- **Submit your top pages:** While most search engines will index the other pages from your website by following links from a page you submit to them, submit the top two or three pages that best summarize your website as well—just in case.
- **Verify and maintain your listing:** Check your pages and ensure they get listed. However, because search engines change their rules, maintaining your listing should be an ongoing task that, once the initial activity has been carried out, needs to be monitored on a monthly basis. Set up a process where essential keywords are established and tested in a number of search engines. Whenever slippage occurs, re-registration should be carried out. However, don't overdo this, as search engines can block sites that are registering too much or too often.

  As a general rule, the top dozen or so search engines account for over 90 percent of search engine-generated traffic. Popular search engines/directories include Yahoo, Google, AltaVista, MSN, Excite, Lycos, Go, Hotbot, All the Web, Direct Hit, LookSmart, Northern Light.

searching tips

Choose a quality search website such as Yahoo, Google, or AltaVista. If you have a very specialist interest, find out if there's a specialist search engine for this type of search.

If you're not getting an appropriate set of results back, try using other keywords or terms. Use a thesaurus to help expand the keywords/terms. Start from the broad and move to the specific. Try to avoid using common words such as "where," "and," "the," as this may result in a very wide set of results being brought back.

Check your spelling. Be careful about American and British English spelling—try both. For example, it's "teleworking" in British English but "telecommuting" in American English. Most search engines are not case sensitive. However, to be comprehensive, try both: "Ireland, ireland."

Put quotation marks around terms, headings, or phrases. The search engine will then search for this exact phrase/term. If you are searching for a specific document, try entering the heading/title of that document. If you're not getting a result, try the author name.

If you want to do advanced search on a search website, spend a few minutes reading the help section.

When using Boolean search commands, remember the key difference between the AND and OR Boolean commands—"Microsoft AND IBM" will search for pages on the Web that have *both* words, "Microsoft" and "IBM." It will exclude pages that have the word "Microsoft" only, or "IBM" only. Using "Microsoft OR IBM" will search for pages with the words "Microsoft" and "IBM," as well as any pages that have "Microsoft" on its own, or "IBM" on its own.

semicolons (;)

Use a semicolon to separate phrases in a list. Use a semicolon to indicate two parallel parts of a sentence:

To err is human; to forgive divine.

Semicolons can get lost on screen, so use them sparingly. If a comma or a period can just as legitimately separate the sentence, use them instead. Semicolons are always outside quotation marks and parentheses.

See also COLONS, QUOTATION MARKS, PARENTHESES AND PUNCTUATION.

sentence spacing

Only one space should be given between sentences.

sentences

The most effective writing style for online reading strives for simplicity. (See ONLINE READER.) Short, simple sentences work best on the Web. Avoid complex sentence constructions that use dependent clauses. For a description of sentence types, see page 9.

server

A server is a computer or device that manages network resources. On the Internet, a server is a computer or program that responds to commands from a client. See also CLIENT.

server logs

Server logs track the number and behavior of readers (visitors) to a website over a specified period. They are generated by server log software. Server logs deliver data such as visitors, unique visitors, page impressions, page views, hits, geographic breakdown, most frequently accessed pages, most frequent paths through a website, etc.

The most common mistake that people make when quoting data from server logs is to use the number of hits instead of page views or visitors. Another potential problem is the amount of data they return. With too much data, there is a danger you will miss the valuable stuff. In configuring a particular server log for a website, you should strip down the log to only the essential data, which will make the process of examining the logs more efficient and beneficial. See HIT, PAGE IMPRESSION, PAGE VIEW.

server side

Occurring on the server side of a client/server system. For example, server-side image maps on Webpages require reference to a separate file on the Web server every time a user clicks an image map. This has an impact both on download times and accessibility. Client-side image maps, in contrast, are executed by the code within the Webpage itself. CGI scripts are server-side applications (they run on the Web server), while JavaScript scripts are client-side (they are executed by your browser). See also ACCESSIBILITY, IMAGE MAP.

SET

Stands for Secure Electronic Transaction, a standard for secure credit card transactions on the Internet.

sexist language

If you use the generic *he*, you risk alienating your readers. We'd recommend not using *he* as a generic or gender-neutral singular pronoun, as in

> If a reader wants to read the page offline, he can print it.

Instead, rewrite the sentence in the plural or in some way that avoids using *he*.

If readers want to read the page offline, they can print it.

If you want to read the page offline, print it.

The use of the third-person plural pronoun *they* to refer to a singular noun or pronoun is quite common in speech and has been used by some notable writers, including W.M. Thackeray and George Bernard Shaw. Be aware, however, that some authorities disapprove and some people consider it wrong (because of the traditional grammatical rule concerning pronoun agreement).

shopping cart

A shopping cart is a common metaphor for the ecommerce software found on a website. Shopping cart software acts as the online catalog and ordering process for a website. It tracks the products individual consumers are intending to buy. Consumers can add or delete items, check the various prices, and complete the purchase if they want to.

site index

See SITE MAP.

site map

A site map, also called a site index, is essentially an index of the classification links used in a particular website. It is generally ordered in an A to Z fashion, thus giving the reader a quick overview of the sections within a website. Sometimes it is presented in a "tree" design, showing how the classifications interlink.

Site maps are especially useful for large websites and, if used, should be part of the global navigation. See also GLOBAL NAVIGATION.

slash

See FORWARD SLASH.

smiley

See EMOTICON.

SMTP

Stands for Simple Mail Transfer Protocol, a protocol for sending and receiving email. Generally, you need to change your SMTP address every time you change your Internet service provider (ISP).

solidus (/)

See FORWARD SLASH.

spacing after period

Use only one space.

spam

Spam is mass-distributed unsolicited email. Day after day, people get emails from organizations or individuals they have never heard of and have absolutely no interest in doing business with, promising everything from get-rich-quick scams to pornographic material. Spam is difficult to ward against and people have quite naturally become sensitive about being spammed.

While the law on spamming is still evolving, anti-spam vigilantes have been known to take matters into their own hands. Organizations that are believed to be consistent spammers have been email "bombed"—huge numbers of emails sent to their email address. Also, there are spam blacklists. If your organization is put on such a blacklist you may find that your emails will not be accepted by a number of other organizations and ISPs. See also EMAIL NEWSLETTER.

special treatment of words (emphasis, irony, etc.)

In traditional publishing, italics or quotation marks are often used to give special expression (emphasis, irony, etc.) to the written word. However, as mentioned in the section on italics, we avoid italics on screen. Also, avoid overuse of quotation marks for emphasis, etc. Remember that emphasis can often best be achieved structurally.

Words and letters used as words and letters should be in italics:

An em dash is the width of the letter *m*.

Kid means goat and *kid* means child.

Italics are not available in many email packages. In this case emphasize a word using asterisks (*):

I was *really* impressed with his speech.

spell checker, spell check

Spell checker (noun), spell check (verb). A program that checks the spelling of words in a document. While spell checkers can catch typos, they do not help when your misspelling creates another valid word; for example, you type *though* instead of *through*. A spell checker is no substitute for a good editor.

The Microsoft Manual of Style opposes the use of *spell check* as a verb, but we would argue that it is now in common use, and the alternative—forcing writers to always use "to check the spelling"—is not feasible. See also WORD PROCESSORS.

spider

A spider is the software used by a search engine to index websites. The spider indexes the pages on a website and then brings that data back to the search engine website where it is compiled into a master index.

splash page

A splash page is an introductory or initial page that is viewed before the actual homepage. Splash pages may be used for navigation reasons, such as when the reader is being asked to choose between a variety of language versions of the website. However, they should never be used from a marketing perspective, whereby some big images or animation are presented to the reader in an attempt to create an "atmosphere" or "feeling." The only feeling such splash pages create with the vast majority of readers is the desire to hit the Back button.

split infinitives

Split infinitives are quite widely used in American English, and examples can be found in the works of many of the finest writers of English prose. Many people, however, have been taught that split infinitives are ungrammatical.

We'd recommend allowing them, but only when to do otherwise would detract from the sentence. Consider the gradations of meaning in the following three phrases:

1 To really like something.
2 Really to like something
3 To like really something.

The first example is clear. The second and third seem to mean something slightly different, and both are awkward. When in doubt about whether to split an infinitive, go with the phrase that sounds right.

SSL

Stands for Secure Sockets Layer, a protocol for transmitting confidential content over the Internet. Used by most ecommerce sites for secure payments.

Sterling

See FOREIGN CURRENCIES.

sticky website

A sticky website keeps readers on the website longer due to compelling content, and keeps them coming back. The objective of most websites should not simply be "stickiness" but to get the busy reader as quickly as possible to the content they need.

story of the day

The "story of the day" should contain the key message that the organization wishes to communicate to its readership on its homepage at any particular point in time. If you look at the front page of a newspaper, one story will dominate. That's because a reader can really only take in one key message at a time.

On the Web, where readers tend to scan read, it's important to grab their attention with a central message that the organization wishes to communicate. See SCAN READING.

streaming

Streaming is a process by which content is delivered in a constant stream. Streaming is most suitable for audio and visual content as these files tend to be large and take a long time to download. (Most text content is small in size and can be downloaded quickly.) Thus, it can be more efficient to play the content as it downloads rather than wait for the entire file to be downloaded and then played. For streaming to work well, a steady and consistent stream needs to be achieved. This is not always possible on the Internet due to bandwidth constraints and the way the Internet is designed.

style guide

A style guide will help establish editorial consistency and correctness throughout your website. Although you should specify a stylebook and reference dictionary to use, you still need to establish your own style guide (no matter how small), even if it lists only your company's spelling of its name and products. There will always be items that are specific to only your company.

Establish which stylebook (such as *The Chicago Manual of Style*) and dictionary you will use as primary and secondary references. List all company product and trademark names. Keep records of anything that has the potential to be inconsistent or wrong—common misspellings, words that have a number of accepted spellings, and so on. State whether you use American or British English, whether you use the serial comma, how you lay out lists, etc.

See the sample style guide in Appendix I for more information.

style sheets

See CSS.

subheads (subheadings)

Short headings inserted roughly every screen and a half (around five paragraphs) that "pull out" a key word, thought, or interesting detail from the text that follows. Subheadings are ideal for scan reading. For tips on their use, see page 7.

sub-homepage

A homepage that is not the main homepage for the organization. If the organization is large, it will have many different sections. Some of these sections will be large enough to require their own website. If not, they will have to be dealt with within the information architecture of the main website.

To deal with these sections properly, it is likely that sub-homepages will have to be developed for each section. Such sub-homepages will contain navigation and content specific to that particular section. They will have their own key messages, their own features. In every other way, a sub-homepage should follow the same best-practice rules as a homepage. See WEBSITE LAYOUT AND DESIGN, INFORMATION ARCHITECTURE.

subscription-based publishing

A subscription service is a method of offering readers access to a restricted part of a website and/or an email publication as a result of their either providing some personal information (an email address, for example) and/or making a financial payment.

Subscription services serve a number of functions. Getting personal information or payment from a reader establishes a firmer relationship with them, which in the casual environment of the Internet is difficult to achieve. You can regularly send them content and not have to wait until they choose to visit your site. The personal information you collect from them enables you to customize and improve your site. While the aim of paid-for subscription services is to generate revenue, with the exception of *The Wall Street Journal*, to date they have not been very successful.

All subscription services should be opt-in (and preferably double opt-in)—the reader should always make the decision to subscribe. Do not send them ads inviting them to subscribe, or subscribe them to one publication just because they have subscribed to another.

Every subscription-based publication should describe clearly what the subscription service offers to the reader, including whether it's free, what it aims to do, what size it will be, how often it will be published, whether it will send other announcements from time to time, what happens to readers' subscription information, and how to subscribe and unsubscribe.

Keep the subscription process as brief as possible. Always verify that someone wants to subscribe to the service by sending a verification message to the email address they have submitted. If the owner of the email address responds to the verification message, then, and only then, can they be subscribed. You should then send a confirmation message, which should include the description outlined above and the email address, username, and password they used to subscribe. See CONFIRMATION MESSAGE, VERIFICATION MESSAGE.

Ensure the unsubscribe process is simple and clear. See UNSUBSCRIBE.

Once a subscriber list begins to build, a situation of "undeliverable addresses" will inevitably occur. Wait a while before unsubscribing these addresses to establish that the problems are not temporary.

It is very important that the subscriber list is properly protected to ensure that it cannot be either stolen or in any way used by spammers or those with malicious intent. Subscriber lists should always be password protected, with access given only to a very few people, and stored on a computer that is either not directly connected to the Internet or which has proper firewall protection. Privacy is one of the most important concerns people have when using the Internet. Having your subscriber list stolen would severely damage trust in your organization and would be a public relations disaster. Back up copies of the subscriber list on a regular basis. Remember, it is a very valuable asset—not something you want to lose.

See also DOUBLE OPT-IN, EMAIL NEWSLETTER, UNSUBSCRIBE.

sub-site

A website that exists within a larger website containing substantial content and is designed in a way to be self-contained. A key impact of a sub-site is on the global navigation, as there will essentially be two "Home" links. A potential way to get around this is to make the overall Home link of the website the name of the organization. For example, "Microsoft Home," "ZDNET.com."

summaries

Web articles that run more than a few screens should include a summary. (For shorter documents, the first paragraph should function as a summary.) It should state briefly what the reader can expect to find in the document, and should include as many key words and phrases as possible. For very long documents, break out the key phrases and show them as hyperlinks—almost like a table of contents—that take the reader directly to the section of interest.

This heading and summary appeared on the homepage of Morgan Stanley Dean Witter in 2000:

> GLOBAL STRATEGY BULLETIN
>
> The latest views of Morgan Stanley Dean Witter strategists and economists worldwide.

While that's respectable, unless potential readers are already familiar with the publication, they may well be guessing as to whether there will be anything of potential interest to them. A more Web-friendly summary, based on the actual document, would be:

> GLOBAL STRATEGY BULLETIN
>
> The latest investment recommendations, economic insights, and stock-market forecasts from Morgan Stanley Dean Witter's renowned strategists and economists. Topics include:
>
> Why the bear market in tech stocks will continue
>
> Which Japanese stocks are bargains today
>
> The case for high-yield US bonds
>
> 5% global growth—the first time since 1973

What investor overconfidence means

Four sectors to avoid this year

Look for a fourth-quarter rally in euro stocks

On a homepage, the summary may need to be shorter than this, depending on the layout and number of articles featured. In a homepage environment, a graphic that is part of a summary should link to the document the summary belongs to. See also WEBSITE LAYOUT AND DESIGN.

support

The Web may well be the world's greatest library. However, there are two key navigation components of a library: a classification system and a human support backup. If you don't know where the history section is or can't find that book on viral marketing, you can always ask someone. In any website, the reader should only be a click away from the ability to contact the organization. Such contact facilities may involve email, telephone, callback, and chat support. You should also supply a "Help" link wherever the reader is faced with carrying out a complex task.

One way to support the reader without human intervention is to structure things in a way that helps them avoid making obvious errors. For example, if the reader is being given a choice of actions, rather than having them type a response, let them choose by clicking or selecting from a set of options.

On the Web, currently the only viable immediate feedback is through text. Text must be used in a comprehensive manner to fully inform the reader of the result of their action. For example, if the reader has filled out a 30-field form and it was not completed successfully, the feedback should isolate the particular error or mistake. It should not say: "Some fields in your form were not filled out correctly." Rather, it should say: "It seems that your email address has not been entered correctly."

Remember, many readers are unfamiliar with the Web, and even those with experience can get reticent, particularly where they are asked to input credit card details, or where they are required to go through a process that is lengthy. Always strive to make the process as simple and foolproof as possible. Explain every single step of the way in precise, straightforward, and friendly language. Use progress chart navigation to show them how much of the process they have completed and how much there is still to complete.

Never underestimate the ability of an average intelligent person to make what often looks to a designer like the most obvious of mistakes. In life, it is often what is most obviously right that we avoid doing, and what is most obviously wrong that we can't help but do. The motto is: "So simple, even an adult can understand it."

See also PROGRESS CHART NAVIGATION.

T

T1, T2, T3

T-carriers are a type of high-capacity digital line generally used to carry voice, data, and other content over long distances. The higher the figure, the larger the capacity of the line. T1 lines are used by many large organizations to connect to the Internet.

table of contents

When a document is long (more than 10 paragraphs), you should provide a table of contents (TOC). Generally it should be placed between the summary and the main body of text, and should be generated from subheads within the documents. In long documents, you should use subheads approximately every five paragraphs. The TOC should be linked to its corresponding subhead within the document. See also WEBSITE LAYOUT AND DESIGN, SUBHEADS.

tables

Traditionally, a table arranges data in rows and columns. Tables are increasingly used to lay out Webpages. Be aware of the accessibility problems this can cause.

Ensure you leave enough space between cells in a table so that the text in the columns is not too close to the next column. See also ACCESSIBILITY.

taxonomy

See CLASSIFICATION.

TCP/IP

The Transmission Control Protocol/Internet Protocol (TCP/IP) is built into the UNIX system and has become the standard for data transmission over networks. It was developed by the US Department of Defense.

techie

A person who is very knowledgeable about technology. Usually someone with programming expertise or background.

tech-savvy

Someone who is computer- and Internet-literate. Also implies someone who is up to date with Internet trends and technological developments.

telecommuting

Also known as teleworking, this is a process where an employee works from home for part or all of the week, while maintaining effective communication with their employer through technology. The Internet supports telecommuting, which is a trend that is gathering some momentum.

telephone numbers

See PHONE/FAX NUMBERS.

Telnet (the program), telnet (the verb)

An Internet protocol that allows users to interact with a remote computer as if directly connected to it.

templates

See CSS.

terabyte

1,099,511,627,776 bytes (1,024 gigabytes), abbreviated TB.

Terms of use statement

A Terms of use statement, which should be accessible from the footer of every page, is useful when you need to cover some or all of the following: Privacy statement; Copyright statement; Software download/use statement (where software is available for download); Trademark statement; Patent statement; License and site access statement; Links to third-party websites statement; Reader-generated content statement (where appropriate); Copyright complaints procedure; Risk of loss (where products are being sold from the website); Product descriptions statement (where products are being sold); Disclaimer of warranties and limitation of liability; and contact information.

Although the Terms of use statement contains the copyright and privacy statements, because these statements are of particular importance on the Web, links to them should be pulled out and also placed in the footer. See also FOOTER.

text color

See COLOR.

that/which

That is defining (tells you something essential about the subject):

> The computer that is in my office is broken. (Not the computer at home)

Which is nondefining or relative (tells you something incidental about the subject).

The computer, which is in my office, is broken. (There's no confusion about which computer is in question, but for your information, it happens to be in my office)

While in British English *that* can often be used in place of *which*, in American English you should always use them in their strict sense.

that/who

Use *who* only when referring to people.

3G

A generic term for the third generation of global wireless communications standards, a technology that will enable high-speed, high-quality transmission of voice, video, and other data. Analog was the first generation of wireless standards and digital was the second generation (see GSM).

There are many questions about the viability of 3G in the short term, not least with regard to the high cost of implementing the infrastructure. Many commentators believe that the high costs will deter the average Web user, who will continue to have limited bandwidth for the foreseeable future. So, from a content perspective, the Web will continue to be driven by low bandwidth content (text and simple images) rather than high bandwidth content (video, animations, audio), for the near future at least.

thumbnail graphic

A small graphic, about the size of a person's thumbnail, that links to a larger version of itself. Used where you want to present a series of graphics, it makes for better presentation and saves significantly on download time.

time of day

Generally, spell out even, half, and quarter hours:

The meeting continued until half past three.

I'll be there by ten o'clock.

Use figures for when you want to emphasize the exact time. Note the colon in American English:

The train leaves at 6:20 A.M.

In British English, a period rather than a colon is used between hour and minute:

6.20 A.M.

When a 24-hour clock is required, use the following style:

04:00

12:00

21:53

See also A.M.

time zones

If you are providing hour and minute information (for example in breaking news) and you have an international readership, you should display the time zone as well. It is also useful to display the time difference between your time zone and Universal Time Coordinated (UTC). UTC is taken as the base time, it is equivalent to GMT. For example

10.22 A.M. EST (UTC -5)

Some common time zones:

European

GMT Greenwich Mean Time, as UTC

WET Western Europe Time, as UTC

CET Central Europe Time, UTC +1

EET Eastern Europe Time, UTC +2

MSK Moscow Time, UTC +3

MSD Moscow Summer Time, UTC +4

US and Canada

AST Atlantic Standard Time, UTC –4

EST Eastern Standard Time, UTC –5

CST Central Standard Time, UTC –6

MST Mountain Standard Time, UTC –7

PST Pacific Standard Time, UTC –8

AKST Alaska Standard Time, UTC –9

HST Hawaiian Standard Time, UTC –10

Australia

AEST Australian Eastern Standard Time, UTC +10

ACST Australian Central Standard Time, UTC +9.5

AWST Australian Western Standard Time, UTC +8

(Often, AST, CST, and WST are used instead, but these time-zone abbreviations could be confusing because they are used in North America as well.)

titles of books, magazines, reports

Capitalize the main words. Use italics for titles of books, films, plays, and long poems, works of art, periodicals (newspapers, magazines, journals, etc.), names of ships. Use regular font (not bold, not italics) in quotation marks for article titles, report titles, chapter titles, shorter poems. See ITALICS, FORMATTING.

titles (of jobs)

Lowercase in general:

> The chief accountant resigned.

titles (of people)

Capitalize the specific president of any country, lowercase a general mention:

> Many admired President Kennedy.
>
> France will elect a president.

TOC

See TABLE OF CONTENTS.

tone

Writing on the Web tends to be less formal than writing for print publication. Treat your readers as though they are as smart as you are, and never talk down to them. But at the same time, don't assume they know everything you know, and don't be overly familiar. On the Web, for instance, a statement such as "The following three points are essential," sounds overly formal. "Here are three important points," would be better. Overuse of the personal pronouns *I*, *me*, *my*, and *mine*—very prevalent on the Web—can make your writing sound amateurish.

Many traditional style guides recommend that you avoid using contractions, such as "It's not what you think," but avoiding them can give writing a stilted quality. The phrase "is he not?," for example, is rarely used in conversation, and seems much more archaic than the familiar "isn't he?". Rudolf Fletch, author of *The Art of Readable Writing* (Hungry Minds, 1994), argued that in this and many other cases, written English should follow conversational custom.

A good rule of thumb is that the tone of your writing should approximate the tone you would use if you were talking to an intelligent stranger.

trademarks

A trademark (™) is a word, device, symbol, or phrase that is used to identify goods made by a company and to distinguish them from those provided by others. A registered trademark (®) is a trademark that has been registered with the relevant authorities, for example the US Patent and Trademark Office.

Do not include trademark symbols on a Webpage (because it affects readability). Instead, a copyright notice such as "Copyright © 1995–2000 Example Company. All rights reserved" should appear in the footer information of every page and link to a separate page for legal information (including trademarks and copyrights). See also FOOTER.

traffic

A term for the number of people who come to a website. If you are referring to the visitors themselves (rather than the number), it is better to call them readers.

Trojan horse

A computer virus that pretends to be an innocuous piece of software or other file in order to get the person to load or activate it.

type color

See COLOR.

typosquatting

Typosquatting is a form of Internet cybersquatting where the typosquatter registers several possible input errors for a popular website, based on the probability that a certain number of people will mistype the website's URL. They then try to sell advertising on the sites that the readers have mistakenly gone to.

U

UK

United Kingdom.

underline

This should be avoided on the Web except for hyperlinks, because readers have been conditioned to think that clicking on underlined text will link them to another part of your document, another document, or another website. See FORMATTING, LINKS.

unique visitor

An individual visitor to a website within a specified time frame. For the unique-visitor measure, repeat visits by that visitor within that time frame are not counted by the site's traffic measurement system. See also HIT.

UNIX

A powerful operating system developed by Ken Thompson and Dennis Ritchie at AT&T Bell Laboratories in 1969.

unsubscribe

The unsubscribe process is the process by which a subscriber is removed from a subscription service. Make sure that the unsubscribe process is simple and clear.

Subscribers should be able to go to a website and enter their email address in a simple form to unsubscribe, and they should also be able to send an email to a special address with an "unsubscribe" instruction.

A common mistake many subscribers make is to forget the email address that they originally subscribed under, and then to try to unsubscribe using their current address. This will obviously result in a failure to unsubscribe. Therefore the following type of statement should be associated with the unsubscribe process:

> Please remember to unsubscribe using the *exact* email address you subscribed with. To find this address, please consult the confirmation message you were sent when you joined the list.

Some subscription software programs have a facility whereby the email address that the subscriber is subscribed with can be published with each newsletter that goes out. This is highly recommended.

If for whatever reason the subscriber does not wish to unsubscribe using the normal channels, they should be able to easily contact someone in the organization, ideally by email, with a request to unsubscribe. Such a request should be treated with the highest priority and they should be unsubscribed immediately.

When someone successfully unsubscribes, they should be sent a "farewell message" informing them that they have been successfully unsubscribed and thanking them for having been a subscriber to the service. See CONFIRMATION MESSAGE.

uppercase, use of

See CAPITALIZATION.

URL

Uniform Resource Locator: the address of a document or site on the Web. Avoid using end punctuation immediately following a URL in body text as the reader might include it when typing it in.

URL navigation

To make it easy for people to navigate to your site using your URL, choose the shortest, most memorable URL possible for the website. If you are aware that readers commonly misspell your URL, register the misspelling, then redirect that URL to the main URL. Choose all lowercase for your URL, as this is what readers are used to seeing. If the website has extensive content in a number of languages, then where possible get a URL for that country (.de for Germany, .ie for Ireland, etc.).

If the website has an extensive range of products, it may make sense to have a number of subsidiary URLs. For example, if you look for the iMac on the Apple website, you will find it under the following URL: www.apple.com/imac/. However, you will also find it under the shorter and more memorable URL: www.imac.com. Both URLs go to the same page.

If you are promoting a certain product or offering, publish the specific URL that will bring the reader to the relevant section on the website rather than the generic homepage. For example, if you're promoting the iMac, you wouldn't point the reader to www.apple.com. Rather, you'd point them to www.imac.com.

Once you've published a page with a specific URL, avoid deleting, moving, or changing the URL for that page, unless the content has gone out of date. If the page is linked to from other websites, the reader will be misdirected, and readers' bookmarks will become invalid. If you do delete a page, try to re-direct the old URL to the most relevant homepage or document. See also NAVIGATION.

US dollars

See FOREIGN CURRENCIES.

USA

United States of America.

usability

From a Web perspective, usability refers to how easy it is for someone to use a website. Web usability examines the ease with which a reader can access pages on the website—whether they download quickly, whether they are compatible with that reader's browser, whether they are accessible to readers with disabilities. It looks at how easy it is to search, and the quality of search results that are returned, as well as how simple it is to navigate through the website. It also looks at how easy it is to complete tasks on the website, such as purchasing a product, getting in touch with the organization, and so on. See also ACCESSIBILITY, INFORMATION ARCHITECT.

Usenet

A worldwide network (available at http://groups.google.com) used as a bulletin board system by special-interest discussion groups. Usenet comprises thousands of newsgroups, each devoted to a particular topic.

user agents

Software to access Web content, including desktop graphical browsers, text browsers, voice browsers, mobile phones, multimedia players, plug-ins, and some software assistive technologies used in conjunction with browsers such as screen readers, screen magnifiers, and voice recognition software.

V

VC

Venture capital: investment funds for high-risk start-up and small businesses with significant potential for growth.

verification message

A verification message email is required to ensure a double opt-in process for subscription services. The verification message informs the receiver that their email address was presented as part of a subscription process. It requests the receiver to reply to the email or click a link to confirm that the receiver does indeed want to subscribe to the said service, or to do neither if they do not wish to subscribe. A verification message ensures that a person is not maliciously subscribed to a service by a third party. See DOUBLE OPT-IN, SUBSCRIPTION-BASED PUBLISHING.

vertical portal

See VORTAL.

viral marketing

Like traditional word of mouth, viral marketing promotes the brand not through direct in-your-face marketing but through getting customers/ readers to positively recommend the brand/product.

An email newsletter is an example of viral marketing if it contains content that readers will quote from and/or pass on to other people they know. Another example of viral marketing is the "email to a friend" facility on a website.

Two classic examples of viral marketing were applied by the Yahoo website and the *Blair Witch Project* film. In the early years, Yahoo spent little or nothing on marketing or advertising. Word of mouth (word of mouse) spread the Yahoo name as people told their friends about the website. With Blair Witch, a website was created that sought to turn fiction into fact. Fans started sending emails to their friends and before long there was a whole communication phenomenon going on.

Viral marketing faces increasing difficulties in an information-overloaded Internet. More than ever, it depends on a "compelling reason to communicate." Yahoo succeeded because it was the first quality website directory. What cemented the viral marketing approach for Yahoo was that millions of websites created links to the Yahoo website because they felt it was a useful resource. Linking is a key component in viral marketing and acts as embedded word of mouth. See LINKS, GETTING LINKED.

virus

A virus contains hidden code that is spread by a host program. It can be harmless but annoying, or quite destructive. One thing to remember about viruses spread by email messages is that they cannot be spread by simply receiving the mail, you need to open the attachment to spread it. So don't open an attachment unless you know the sender and know for sure that it is from the sender. Even then, be careful, be mindful that some viruses, such as the Love Bug, can come from the mailbox of somebody you know. If in doubt, send them an email first to enquire whether the attachment is actually from them. See also LOVE BUG.

visit

A single access of a website by a reader.

visitor

Somebody who visits a website over a defined period. A visitor may have visited a website a number of times during this period. A unique visitor counts as a particular visitor only once, no matter how many times they have come back during the period in question. See UNIQUE VISITOR.

vortal

Also known as a vertical portal, a vortal is a portal website that provides comprehensive information to a specific industry or interest group. See also PORTAL.

W3

Another word for the World Wide Web.

W3C

Short for World Wide Web Consortium, an international consortium of commercial and educational institutions that seeks to promote common standards and interoperability on the Web. The W3C was founded in 1994 by Tim Berners-Lee, the original architect of the World Wide Web.

WAN

Stands for wide area network, a network that connects geographically separated areas.

WAP

Wireless Application Protocol, a technology standard that allows mobile/cell phone users to access limited Internet content. WAP was hugely hyped for its potential for mcommerce (mobile commerce), but it hasn't yet lived up to its expectations. Because of small screens, poor technology, cost, and usability issues, very few people have participated in WAP-enabled services. See also i-mode.

Web, Web

An abbreviation for the World Wide Web. Capitalize when referring to the noun:

> The Web is a useful research tool.

Lowercase when using as an adjective:

> web users

Web address

Also known as a URL. What the reader types in the address field of their browser to go to a particular website. For example, www.oracle.com.

While it's sufficient to use the shortened address in browsers, if you are sending a Web address to someone by email—and particularly if you are sending out an email newsletter to a large group of subscribers—always include the "http://" as some programs won't translate it into a link without it (http://www.oracle.com). If the URL is more than 65 characters long, place it in angle brackets (<>). See URL, URL navigation.

Web browser

Software application that displays Webpages. The most popular are Microsoft Internet Explorer and Netscape Navigator.

Webmaster

In the early days of the Web, the Webmaster was the jack of all trades who did everything from designing, coding, writing and editing to marketing, and maintaining the website. As websites evolved it became impossible for one person to do all these things. The term Webmaster has thus become a slightly confused term. It is still used to refer to people in charge of smaller websites, but in larger ones, it generally refers to someone responsible for the technical maintenance of the website. See also MANAGING EDITOR, INFORMATION ARCHITECT.

Webpage

One word. See PAGE.

Webpage design

See WEBSITE LAYOUT AND DESIGN.

website

One word (often shortened to "site"). A website is a publication. It is a place where a reader comes primarily to read content. The role of a website is to deliver the right content to the right reader at the right time at the right cost to further the objectives of the organization. These objectives may include getting the reader to purchase a product online, and/or getting the reader to get in touch with the organization with a view to purchasing a product.

website layout and design

See Section II, "Designing for the Web," for an overview of this area.

Quality website design creates simple, easy-to-read, fast-downloading pages, while also providing a quality navigation and search, and establishing a sense of style (there are a lot of elements at play on any one Webpage, good design makes it all look stylish and coherent).

- **Page layout and design:** Page layout should be optimized for 800-pixel width to ensure maximum compatibility. (The design width should actually be 760 pixels to allow for the scroll bar on the right.)

  Scrolling is preferable to repeated clicking. However, pages should ideally be no more than three screens and a maximum of six. Homepages should ideally be two screens or less. A reader should only have to scroll vertically. They should never have to scroll horizontally.

  Global navigation should appear consistently on every page. (See GLOBAL NAVIGATION, NAVIGATION.) Avoid presenting text as a graphic, unless that text is part of a navigation graphic or banner ad. Substantial quantities of text (a paragraph or more) should never be presented as a graphic, as this slows the download of the page and does not deliver any significant benefit to the reader. It also creates accessibility problems.

All Webpages should contain a masthead and footer. See MASTHEAD, FOOTER. All Webpages should contain a basic search function either in the right of the masthead or near the top left of the page, underneath the organization logo. See SEARCH.

Use a three-column layout on homepages.

- **Homepage layout and design:** The most critical part of a homepage is the "first screen" that the person sees when they arrive at the page. Make sure that the key content and navigation are always viewable from the first screen. Absolutely avoid SPLASH PAGES.

  Remember, a key function of any homepage is to promote important content to the reader. Headings and summaries are an effective way of doing this. In most print media there is a central "story of the day" that the publication leads with. This is to grab the reader's attention. Basically, media experts have found that it's easier to grab someone's attention by putting in front of them one compelling story (perhaps underpinned by a few stories of lesser prominence) than to present several stories, each with the same level of presentation importance.

  It is recommended that you have at least one heading and full summary, but no more than five. These headings and full summaries should be placed in the center column. Headings with one-line summaries, or headings on their own, can be placed underneath the heading and full summary, or in the right column.

  When the heading is in a heading-and-summary environment, it should always be a link to the full document because this is what the reader expects, due to their familiarity with search processes where the heading/title is always a link to the full document. Provide a date at the beginning of the summary (see DATING DOCUMENTS AND SUMMARIES). At the end of the full summary, there should be a link denoting "More" or "Full Story." The heading and summary should carry through to the relevant document page. If there is an image associated with the heading and summary, it should link through to the same page. The image itself should also carry through. See Figure 3.16.

FIGURE 3.16

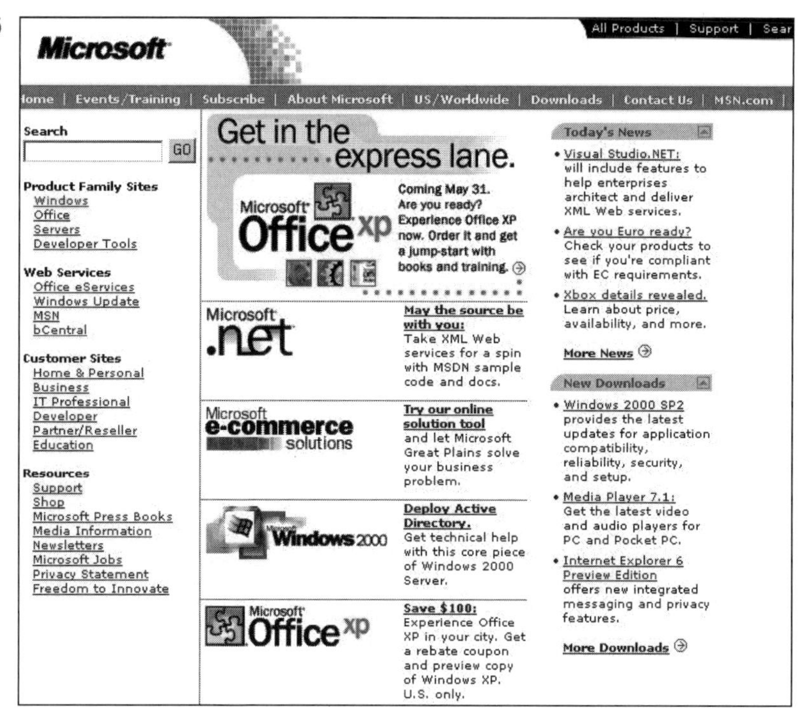

The Microsoft homepage is an example of good, crisp layout.

- **Document layout and design:** Pages that display documents should ideally follow the three-column approach (see COLUMN), with the body of the document in the center column (see Figure 3.17). Where there are large images, tables, or diagrams involved, it may be appropriate to drop the right column. However, care needs to be taken that the images are not too large, from a download or print perspective. Avoid any image so wide it forces the reader to scroll horizontally. If the image requires viewing in a larger format, consider placing a smaller version of it within the document, then linking to the larger version on a page of its own. If doing this, state the file size of the image.

FIGURE 3.17

IrishExaminer.com — Tuesday, August 7, 2001 | Home

IRELAND | WORLD | SPORT | BUSINESS | OPINION | SUPPLEMENTS | BREAKING NEWS | WEEK IN NEWS

Home > Full Story

Advanced Search

NEWS

IRELAND
SPORT
BUSINESS
WORLD
OPINION

SUPPLEMENTS

ARENA
CONNECT
FARMING
FEELGOOD
FOOD
PROPERTY

SERVICES

ATTITUDE
BULLETIN BOARD
CHAT
CONTACTS
EDIT MY DETAILS
FAMILY NOTICES
HELP
HOROSCOPES
MEDIA PACK
ON THIS DAY
PRIVACY POLICY

August 7, 2001

Palestinians refuse to arrest seven men on Israel's most-wanted list

By Jeffrey Heller

THE Palestinian Authority refused yesterday to arrest any of the seven men on an Israeli most-wanted list that could mark them for death under a widely condemned hunt-and-kill policy.

Palestinian Information Minister Yasser Abed Rabbo said Israel must first take action against its own militants before the Authority could consider demands to detain the seven Palestinians.

"The Israeli government should arrest 50 persons - armed settlers -- who are active as terrorists and killers," he said, citing the killing last month by suspected Jewish vigilantes of three Palestinians including a baby boy.

Releasing its list on Sunday, the Israeli Defence Ministry said the seven men, from several Palestinian factions, "continue to carry out attacks" despite Israeli appeals to the Palestinian Authority to arrest them and other activists.

Ireland
10:27:51 AM
Trimble rejects proposals, Suspension of Assembly looms

Sport
10:25:33 AM
Athletics: Drugs failure cause championship embarrassment

World
10:44:31 AM
Tourist gives birth on holiday bus

Business
10:02:10 AM
Slide in telecoms stocks hits Footsie

Main Topics
Northern peace process

More Breaking News

SUPPLEMENTS

click here for the connect section sponsored by:
eircom.ie

An example of the document layout approach used by IrishExaminer.com

Specific document layout guidelines include

- using sans serif fonts such as Arial or Verdana in 10-point (see FONTS)
- using black text on an 85 percent white background (see COLOR)
- dating the document at the very top of the document (see DATING DOCUMENTS AND SUMMARIES)
- providing a heading for every document (see HEADINGS)
- providing a byline, linked to a biography or an email contact form (see BYLINE)
- providing a summary or introductory paragraph (see SUMMARIES)
- having between 9 and 12 words per line for the document text, as this optimizes readability (see LINE LENGTH)
- using pull quotes to facilitate scan reading (see PULL QUOTES)

- providing an "email this" and "print this" facility (see EMAIL TO A FRIEND, PRINTING)
- providing a copyright notice at the end of every document, as well as the copyright link in the footer of the page (see COPYRIGHT)

When a document is long (more than 10 paragraphs), provide a table of contents (TOC), and place it in between the summary and the main body of text. The TOC should be generated from subheads within the documents. In long documents, use subheads every four to five paragraphs. The TOC should be linked to its corresponding subhead within the document.

When a document is longer than 30 paragraphs, or 1,500 words of text, as well as providing the table of contents, break up the document into separate pages at least every 1,000 words, or 20 paragraphs. Provide details on how many pages there are. Ideally this should be given at the top and bottom of the page. It should be presented in a "1-2-3-4" format (see Figure 3.18). Each of the page numbers should be hyperlinked to the appropriate page, except for the page being viewed, which should be unlinked. There should also be a "Previous page" link (on all but the first page) and "Next page" link (on all but the last page). At the bottom of each page it's important to encourage the reader to click to the next page. A practical way of doing this is to place the first subheading from the next page beside the "Next page" link. It should be a link but should link to the top of the next page, not to the subheading itself.

FIGURE 3.18

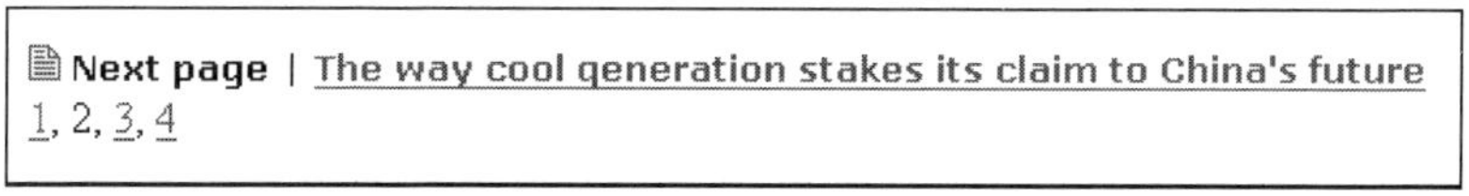

Next page | The way cool generation stakes its claim to China's future
1, 2, 3, 4

An example of a page number approach by Salon.com

Documents without graphics can look bare and intimidating. While it is important to ensure that the page downloads quickly, a quality graphic can sometimes help the reader better understand the information that is being communicated.

A graphic should usually be right-aligned or horizontal across the column (left-aligned can cause accessibility problems). A good place for them to appear is at the top of the document, underneath the heading. A graphic should not dominate the screen.

If the graphic has a different copyright from the document, the copyright information should appear before the descriptive text. If the copyright notice is already embedded in the graphic, there's no need to repeat the information. Follow the normal rules for graphics. See GRAPHICS.

white space

White space aids scannability. At least 20 percent of your screen should be made up of white space (blank). See also COLOR.

window

A single copy of the browser. You can open a second browser window or more by selecting the file function in most browsers. It allows the reader to have a number of browsers open at the same time.

Don't force the browser to open another browser window when a reader selects a link unless you have a very good reason. It irritates the reader because it removes some of their control and seems to disable the Back button. Forcing them to open a second window will not force them to stay on your site, and is more likely to backfire as readers get annoyed.

WIPO

The World Intellectual Property Organization rules on domain-name disputes.

wired

A wired building or organization is equipped for the Internet. A wired person is a regular user of the Internet.

word processors

Always write and edit text in a good word-processing package with spell-check and search facilities before you transfer it to HTML. It's a lot more difficult to edit text that is surrounded by code.

While spell checkers can catch typos, they do not help when your mis-spelling creates another valid word—for example, you type *though* instead of *through*. A spell checker is no substitute for a good editor.

Use the word count facility available in packages such as Microsoft Word to check the length of your lines and paragraphs. You'll find it on the Tools menu. Average paragraph length on the Web should be no longer than 50 words, while lines should be narrower than 12 words (about 70 spaces).

Another useful tool for editing is the Track Changes facility in Word. It allows both the writer and editor to track all changes within a document and accept or reject those changes as required. This is also found on the Tools menu, select Tools > Track Changes > Highlight Changes, and select the Track Changes while Editing checkbox and click OK (in Microsoft Word 2000)—see Figure 3.19.

FIGURE 3.19

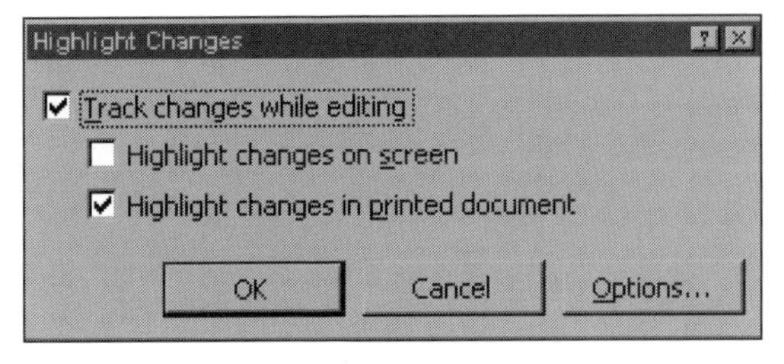

The Track Changes facility in Word is a useful tool.

All changes to the document will be easily identifiable by the use of different colors. If you want to see the text without the edits highlighted, simply deselect the Highlight changes on screen checkbox.

When reviewing a document that has been edited with the Track Changes feature activated, simply right-click a change to display a shortcut menu where you can either accept or reject that change. If you select the Accept or Reject Changes option in this menu you can also choose to accept or reject all changes without review.

World Wide Web

More commonly referred to simply as the Web. See WEB.

writing guidelines

See Section I, "Writing for the Web," for detailed guidelines on this topic. Here are a few reminders:

- **Style:** Be concise. Use positive rather than negative statements. Write simply and naturally, avoiding jargon.
- **Use effective headings:** They should be punchy and descriptive. Make them brief, direct, and meaningful. Use the active voice (this gives the heading more impact):

  Europe is dying

  not

  The death of Europe

  Use keywords (this helps the readers to scan your text and allows it to be found in a search engine). Don't deceive the reader or assume that the reader will know anything about the document.
- **Use effective summaries:** They should "sell" your document. Use keywords from the document. Include the main points from the article, the who, what, where, when, how. Use vivid or forceful words and phrases.
- **Use short paragraphs:** Text should be broken into short, manageable paragraphs (five lines or less) and each line should contain a maximum of 12 words. Format the paragraphs appropriately, introducing subheadings, links, bullet points, and tables.

WYSIWYG

Pronounced "wizziwig"—"what you see is what you get."

X

XML

Extensible Markup Language, an emerging standard for presenting information on the Internet. Unlike HTML, which simply describes how content should be displayed, XML allows developers to customize tags so that the content can be identified and described. For example, if a document contains a byline, bio, summary, and date of publication, XML tags can be created to define these.

A major advantage of XML is that it significantly improves the reader's ability to do an advanced search. For example, if documents have been tagged with XML tags detailing author name, a reader can get a very accurate set of search results by a particular author. Without XML tags, if they did such a search they would get results relating to documents an author had written, but also any other documents that might have mentioned this author. See also METADATA.

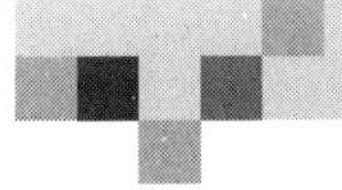

Y

years

Years are expressed in figures, but avoid starting a sentence with a figure (see NUMBERS). Rephrase instead. For punctuation and layout of years in dates, see DATES.

Z

ZIP codes

All capitals. When requesting ZIP codes in forms, remember that some of your readers may not have ZIP in the countries they live in. Either do not make the ZIP compulsory, or else inform the reader that they should write "None" in the ZIP field if they don't have such a code.

APPENDIX I: SAMPLE STYLE GUIDE

The following is an example of a basic style guide:

WebWorks Style Guide

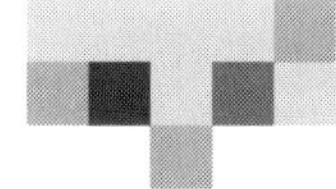

LANGUAGE

The language we use in all WebWorks content is American English.

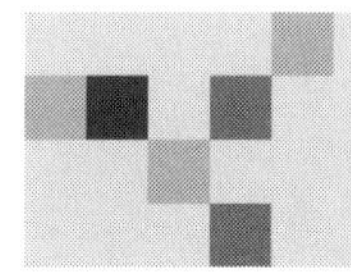

REFERENCE DICTIONARIES AND STYLEBOOKS

All writers and editors should consult our main reference dictionary, *The American Heritage Dictionary of the English Language, 4th edition*, and our main stylebook, *The Chicago Manual of Style, 14th edition*, when querying spelling or usage.

If these do not provide the answers use *Webster's New World Collegiate Dictionary, 10th edition, The New York Times Manual of Style and Usage*, *The Associated Press Stylebook and Briefing on Media Law* as secondary sources.

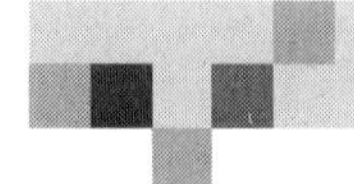

USAGE

Comma

Use the serial comma (the final comma before the *and* in a series of three or more items).

The colors in the American flag are red, white, and blue.

Dash

Use an unspaced em dash (—).

The physical impediment will lessen—perhaps even disappear—in time.

Order of punctuation

Periods and commas are always inside quotation marks.

Possessives

Form the possessive of a singular noun ending in *s* by adding an *'s*:

Charles's *not* Charles'

Ellipsis

Use three dots (...) for an ellipsis, whether a sentence has been left out or not. Always provide a space either side of the ellipsis.

Abbreviations/contractions

Abbreviations that are formed by using the first initials of separate words should not have any periods after the letters:

USA

No periods are needed after words that are shortened by using at least their first and last letters, for example:

Mr, Ltd, Dept

Numbers

Spell out numbers up to and including nine. Don't start a sentence with a figure, spell out or rephrase.

Round numbers can be both digits and words: thousands normally in digits, millions in words. Use commas in four-digit number and upwards:

1,000, 10,000

Dates

Lay out dates as follows:

Thursday, May 3, 2001

Capitalization style in headings

Use initial capitalization only (capitalize the first word and proper nouns only) in headings.

Tech stocks slump again

WebWorks releases WebWorks Pro

WORD LIST/GLOSSARY

WebWorks terms

WebWorks (the company name—note the capital W in the middle of the name)

WebWorks Pro

WebWorks Lite

We have *customers* not *clients*.

General terms

AltaVista

dotcom

ebusiness

Internet

intranet

keyword

techie (not "tekkie")

webpage

website

FURTHER READING/ONLINE RESOURCES

Style and writing guides

- *The Chicago Manual of Style: The Essential Guide for Writers, Editors, and Publishers*, 14th Edition, preface by John Grossman, University of Chicago Press, 1993

  This guide is not available online, but an FAQ page is available at www.press.uchicago.edu/Misc/Chicago/cmosfaq.html

- *The Associated Press Stylebook and Briefing on Media Law*, by Norm Goldstein (editor) *et al.*, Associated Press, 2000.

- *The Oxford Dictionary for Writers and Editors: The Essential Guide for Anyone Who Works With Words*, 2nd edition, Oxford University Press, 2000.

- *The New York Times Manual of Style and Usage: The Official Style Guide Used by the Writers and Editors of the World's Most Authoritative Newspaper*, by Allan M. Siegal and William G. Connolly, Times Books, 1999.

- *The Columbia Guide to Online Style*, by Todd Taylor and Janice Walker, Columbia University Press, 1998.

- *The Careful Writer: A Modern Guide to English Usage*, by Theodore M. Bernstein, Free Press, 1995.

- *The Elements of Style*, by William Strunk Jr *et al.*, Allyn and Bacon, 2000.
- *The American Heritage Book of English Usage: A Practical and Authoritative Guide to Contemporary English*, by editors of The American Heritage Dictionaries, Houghton Mifflin Company, 1996.

  Available online at www.bartleby.com
- Orwell's rules in "Politics and the English Language" in *Collected Essays Journalism and Letters: In Front of Your Nose, 1945–1950: The Collected Essays, Journalism & Letters*, Vol. 4, by George Orwell, edited by Ian Angus and Sonia Orwell, David R. Godine, 2000
- The US Government Printing Office, Style Manual 2000 online:

  www.access.gpo.gov/styleman/2000/browse-sm-00.html
- Bartleby.com has a full searchable database of reference guides, encyclopedias, and much more. Just some of the works you'll find here include *The American Heritage Dictionary of the English Language*, *Fowler's Modern English Usage*, *The Elements of Style*, and *The American Heritage Book of English Usage*.

  www.bartleby.com
- Content Exchange bills itself as the "digital marketplace for online writers, editors, and publishers." In addition to putting publishers and writers in touch with each other, it provides quite a good newsletter focusing on web content.

  www.content-exchange.com
- Edit-Work.com is designed to help online editors and provides some useful tips on creating a style guide and establishing editorial procedures.

  www.edit-work.com
- This guide to grammar and writing, maintained by Professor Charles Darling of Capital Community College, Hartford, Connecticut, is a comprehensive grammar site with a particularly useful "ask grammar" service.

  http://ccc.commnet.edu/grammar/

American dictionaries

- *The American Heritage Dictionary of the English Language*, 4th edition, by editors of The American Heritage Dictionaries, Houghton Mifflin Company, 2000.

  Available online at www.bartleby.com

- *Merriam Webster's Collegiate Dictionary*, 10th edition, by Merriam Webster, Merriam Webster, 1998.

  Available online at www.m-w.com

British dictionaries

- *The New Oxford Dictionary of English*, Judy Pearsall and Patrick Hanks (eds), Oxford University Press, 1999.

Technology dictionary

- Webopedia—Online dictionary and search engine for technical terms.

  www.webopedia.com

Web design

- *Designing Web Usability: The Practice of Simplicity*, by Jakob Nielsen, New Riders Publishing, 2000.

  Jakob Nielsen's usability website, www.useit.com, is a mine of essential usability information.

- *Web Style Guide: Basic Design Principles for Creating Web Sites*, by Patrick J. Lynch and Sarah Horton, Yale University Press, 1999.

  Available online at http://info.med.yale.edu/caim/manual/contents.html

- *Content Critical: Gaining Competitive Advantage Through High-Quality Web Content*, by Gerry McGovern and Rob Norton, Financial Times Prentice Hall, 2001.

- The World Wide Web Consortium's (W3C) guidelines on web content accessibility.

  www.w3.org/TR/WCAG10/

- Search Engine Watch provides a comprehensive guide to search engine registration and optimization.

  www.searchenginewatch.com

- Usable Web is a collection of links about information architecture and user interface issues specific to the Web.

  http://usableweb.com/

QUICK-FIND INDEX

Grammar and usage

abbreviations and acronyms 33
capitalization 52
collective nouns 58
consistency 65
contractions 68
dates 75
ellipsis 91
foreign currencies 103
italics 130
language 134
lists 140
measurements/symbols 145
months 149
numbers 163
parentheses and punctuation 171
phone/fax numbers 175
prepositions to watch 177
quotations 185
referencing online sources 188
sexist language 200
special treatment of words 202
spell checker, spell check 203
split infinitives 204
style guide 205
that/which 212
time of day 213
time zones 214

Punctuation

colons 58
comma 60
dash 73
hyphens 119
possessives 177
semicolons 199

Writing and editing

See Section I: Writing for the Web
bylines 51
calendar of events 51
collaborative content 57
commissioning content 63
content acquisition 65
corrections 71
editing content 89
email writing 95
fact-checking 98
headings 115
online reader 165
Orwell's rules 167
style guide 205
subheads 206
summaries 208
tone 216

word processors 231
writing guidelines 232

Online reader

information overload 125
online reader 165
reader identification 187
scan reading 190
server logs 200
usability 220

Document layout guidelines

Main entry: Document layout and design section in Website layout and design
dating documents and summaries 77
fonts 102
formats 105
formatting 105
graphics within documents 114
line length 139
page numbers 169
paragraphs 171
pull quotes 183
sentences 199
table of contents 210

Marketing and advertising

Main entry: promoting content
advertorial 36
banner ad 45
branding 48
email mailing list 91
email marketing 92
email newsletter 92
email signature 95
getting linked 110
hit 116
offline promotion 164
search engine registration and optimization 197
subscription-based publishing 206
viral marketing 221

Navigation

Main entry: navigation
classification 54
classification path navigation 55
core navigation 70
document navigation 82
drop-down navigation 85
ecommerce/shopping-cart navigation 88
global navigation 111
homepage navigation 117
language and geographic navigation 137
personalization 174
progress chart navigation 180
related navigation 188
URL navigation 219

Interaction

chat 53
discussion board 81
email mailing list 91
feedback 100
moderator 148
online community 165
reader-generated content 187
subscription-based publishing 206
support 209

Website layout and design

Main entry: Website layout and design as well as Section II: Designing for the Web
accessibility 34
classification 54
feedback 100
Flash 102
fonts 102
footer 102
forms 106
frames 108
graphics 113
information architect 123
link title 139
links 139
logos 142
masthead 144
metadata 147
multimedia 151
navigation 151
non-HTML documents 163
page downloads 168
page length 169
PDF 173
personalization 174
printing 179
screen size 191
scroll 192
site map 201
splash page 203
streaming 205
tables 210

Search

Main entry: search
keyword 133
metadata 147
metatag 147
search directory 195
search engine 196
search engine registration and optimization 197
searching tips 198

Legal

attribution 42
copyright 70
corrections 71
fact checking 98
libel 138
plagiarism 175
privacy 179
Terms of use statement 212
trademarks 216

Functions and roles

copyeditor 69
editor 90
editorial board 90
information architect 123
managing editor 143
moderator 148
webmaster 224

Issues of concern

best viewed with 46
broadband 49
circular linking 54
color, colour 59
Flash 102
fonts 102
frames 108
graphics 113
italics 130
page counter 168
page downloads 168
PDF 173
plagiarism 175
privacy 179
spam 202
splash page 203
underline 218

Information economy terms

content 65
content management 67
data 74
data management 75
digital age 81
digital divide 81
extranet 98
information 122
information economy 124
information literate 124
information overload 125
intellectual capital 125
Internet 126
intranet 128
knowledge 133
knowledge capital 133
knowledge management (KM) 134
new economy 162
publishing 182